The Power of Resourcefulness

How a career coach navigated a
successful career transition
across continents

Esiher Wang

Author: Esther Wang

Title: The Power of Resourcefulness

Papaerback ISBN: 979-8-9989905-2-6

Ebook ISBN: 979-8-9989905-1-9

Published by Beacon Career

To the people, animals, mountains, and rivers that have accompanied me on this journey of transition.

Contents

Author's Note

The last time I wrote an author's note was in December 2018, in Shanghai, for my first book, *Awakening: Design Your Life to Be the Way You Want (Chinese version)*. That book was about how I helped my clients navigate their career development and career transitions as a career coach.

Now, I am writing the author's note for my second book, my first English book. This time, the story is different. This book is about how I helped myself through my biggest career and life transitions—as an immigrant in the U.S. and as a career coach.

In my mind, a good coach not only helps others but walks the journey themselves, living as the person they truly want to be. That belief has fueled me for the past fifteen years.

From East to West.

From China to the U.S.

From being a career coach in China to becoming an international career coach serving clients in the U.S.

From coaching solely in Chinese to embracing my role as a bilingual coach in both Chinese and English.

From being a Chinese entrepreneur to an American entrepreneur.

From a Chinese author to an English author.

This journey of transition took nearly four years. Even now, I am still on this journey.

I know many highly educated immigrants who come to the U.S. in their twenties, thirties, and even forties, only to find themselves needing to change career paths, sometimes from white-collar to blue-collar jobs, due to language and cultural barriers. I didn't give up!

I arrived in the U.S. in 2019 at thirty-nine years old. Six months later, the pandemic hit. My career transition collided with this global crisis. I followed William Bridges' transition model for this major career and life transition. William Bridges was an American author, speaker, and organizational consultant best known for his work on transition and change management.

His transition model offers a powerful framework for understanding the emotional and psychological journey people experience during transition. It outlines three stages:

1. Endings: letting go of the old way or identity.

2. The Neutral Zone: a period of uncertainty and adjustment.

3. A New Beginning: embracing new roles, goals, or identity.

Bridges emphasized that transition is internal, and managing this emotional process is key to navigating change successfully.

My journey has moved through each of these three stages. I spent two years in the Ending stage. Pausing my Chinese business took real courage, and endings always require bravery. Fear was my biggest obstacle. Looking back, I have to say that, in some ways, the pandemic supported me in making that hard decision.

Then, I entered the Neutral Zone, which lasted another two years. This was truly a priceless time for me. Stepping into my forties was the first time in my life I had allowed myself such a long break. During this stage, I explored happiness, practiced emotional release, untangled negative connections with my birth country, and deepened my relationship with myself. I volunteered so that I could better understand the American people and tapped into industry associations to build peer coaching relationships. In this space, I emptied the past and made room to nurture a new future.

Now, in the New Beginning stage, I still face many challenges. But what I do is simple: take action. In this phase, you will feel a deep sense of necessity, a stripping away to reveal your most authentic self. This was one of the biggest surprises and gifts of this journey. Luckily, I found my necessity at the New Beginning stage.

At each stage, I share with you the challenges I faced and how I moved through them—using professional knowledge, external resources, and, most importantly, the biggest resource of all: my inner world.

Through coaching support and daily practices like mantras, meditation, journal work, and emotional release, I created many visualizations about my future and my self-image. Sometimes, I saw myself as a giant flower, Titan Arum, symbolizing my growth journey, slowly blooming in my own time. Other times, I became Maleficent, a powerful fairy from Disney's movie *Maleficent*, played by Angelina Jolie, representing my Western feminine power, flying through the sky with powerful wings. I felt the black panther within me—my masculine strength—moving confidently through the African grasslands to hunt and fight. I also saw Cora-line, who is a brave and curious young girl from the movie *Cora-line*, in me, my young American girl version, starting an adventurous journey with her black cat.

I imagined an English manor with wide, open lands repre-senting my business map—grounded, stable, and expansive. I saw myself as a white horse, my spiritual self, her shining mane flowing as she ran freely toward me. I became a blue whale, symbolizing my international expansion, setting off from the American shore into the vast ocean. And sometimes, I was the Kenai River in Alaska, calm, flowing, and abundant, representing financial peace.

These visualizations helped me create a new future and let go of my outdated identities. They brought joy and clarity to my new career in the U.S.

Whenever I faced hardship, I went inward. That's where I found strength, insight, and creative solutions. This journey has helped me rediscover my resourcefulness, and I deeply believe that everyone is resourceful inside. Your true self is always there, waiting. The guidance you need is already within you.

If you're in the middle of a big transition, career, life, or both, please trust this process. It's not a detour. It's your soul's big gift.

As it says in *The Alchemist*:

"When you truly desire something, all the universe conspires to help you achieve it."

Respecting Identities

Throughout this book, I've shared my personal journey and my work as a career coach. To protect the privacy and dignity of others, I have taken thoughtful steps to safeguard their identities.

Some names are real and used with permission. Others have been changed or are represented with pseudonyms to preserve anonymity. Coaching clients are not named, and identifying details have been omitted or altered. In some cases, organizational names have also been replaced with fictional ones to maintain confidentiality and avoid misrepresentation.

While the stories and reflections in this book are true to my journey, every effort has been made to honor the privacy and trust of those involved.

Part One
Ending

Chapter 1
Where Was My Green Card?

O n July 5th, 2019, just one day after U.S. Independence Day, I landed at Dallas Fort Worth International Airport to present customs with my immigration documents—the passport with the immigrant visa, a sealed envelope containing my medical exam results, a copy of my birth certificate, police clearance certificates, and more.

As required, I had completed my medical examination back in March at a hospital in Shanghai approved by the U.S. Citizenship and Immigration Services (USCIS). The results were sent directly into the sealed envelope, and I never saw them myself.

I was thirty-nine years old and at the peak of my career. Behind me was the coaching business I had built in Shanghai, where I led a dedicated team of six women and created a strong foundation. Leaving that life behind was not a decision I made lightly—it was deeply personal and connected to a journey that had started years earlier.

Let me give you a short introduction to why I immigrated to the U.S. In 2013, I attended an eighteen-month "Fighting with the Poor" volunteer program, and I spent one year in the U.S. and six months in Malawi, a small country next to South Africa. During this program, I experienced the U.S. as better: big land, freedom, rights, driving freely, and friendly people. Also, I knew my current husband, Mike, who was British and a staff member of the organization where I volunteered, called One World Center in Michigan. Furthermore, we developed an intimate relationship.

After I finished this program, I went to Shanghai to establish my own business: career coaching. Finally, Mike followed me to Shanghai, and he found a math teacher position at an international high school there. In 2016, we got married in Shanghai. Through our marriage therapist, who was from Australia, we knew Mike could apply for a U.S. Green Card for me, as Mike was a green card holder.

I passed my immigration interview on April 28th at the U.S. Consulate General in Guangzhou. Outside the Consulate, Mike and I hugged and wept—we knew we were about to begin a new chapter in our lives.

After spending a year in the U.S., I realized something important: this country truly aligned with my core value—freedom. When I completed the volunteer program in May 2015, I told myself that I would come back and make the U.S. my permanent home.

Four years later, I did.

Then Mike found a teaching job in Charlotte, and he came in June. I needed to deal with all the stuff for the Shanghai apartment, so I joined him later.

The customs officer took the package, put it aside carelessly, and stamped my passport. He was more casual than the other customs officers.

In a short moment, he told me:

"It is done!"

A thought flashed through my mind:

"He is not very serious, and I hope he will not lose my green card stuff."

My thought became a reality in the following months. I was busy with my business: career coaching for individuals, training independent career coaches, and supplying online courses for self-development and career development. All the operations were online. I didn't tell any friends and clients that I had immigrated to the U.S. Only my family and team members knew.

Most new immigrants choose not to tell other people about their immigration for the first few years. It is for the safety of their careers, especially if they still need to continue to work in their birth country.

I lived in the U.S., but my heart was with China, and my working time also followed the Chinese time shift. There is a twelve-hour time difference between China and Charlotte from March to November and a thirteen-hour difference during the winter months. When my Chinese team started their workday in the morning, it was evening for me. I usually held meetings, trainings, and coaching sessions in the early morning or late evening.

Every Friday evening, I was so happy because in China it was Saturday, and my team and I didn't need to work. But Sunday nights became my struggling time—I needed to work, as it was Chinese Monday morning. It was very hard to change that energy. I thought I might need to start my American career, but I did not have the time and confidence for that.

Three months passed, and I still hadn't received my Green Card. We gave Mike's friend's address for receiving a Green Card. Then I went to the USCIS website to check the process, and it showed that it had been delivered three weeks earlier. Mike contacted his friend, and she said that they had never received the Green Card. We considered filing a suit, but it wouldn't help us find the missing package. It was sent via USPS, not UPS, and it was very hard to track.

We applied for a new one. We filled out a new form, and it took several months until we got a reply: the payment was unsuccessful. We had to start a new process. When I needed to travel outside the U.S. (to the UK and China), I went to the USCIS Charlotte Field Office to get a temporary I-551 stamp in my passport, which served as proof of my Green Card status.

We settled in Charlotte, which is a very beautiful city. I felt very lucky when I found out Charlotte was called The Queen City, as my English name, Esther, came from a queen's name in the Bible. I was Queen Esther and lived in a queen city. That was so great.

Most of the time, we had sunny days. Even in the winter, the weather was not very cold. We chose Charlotte because we wanted to find a sunny and warm city. It rained a lot in Shanghai, and it was very cold in the winter. Also, we wanted to be on the East Coast, as there was a twelve-or thirteen-hour difference from China, and it was easy to do my Chinese business.

We like Charlotte. There are many trees, and we like to hike the Little Sugar Creek Greenway, which is nineteen miles long and runs through the city. In spring, flowers bloom everywhere. In summer, we go camping and enjoy the beach. In fall, we drive along the Blue Ridge Parkway to admire the colorful leaves. And in winter, we can go skiing.

When I had time, I went to ESL (English as a Second Language) classes. I thought it was a great way to improve my English. I searched online and found ESL lessons at a big local church. I registered for the lesson, and for the first time, everyone had to take an oral test of their English proficiency level.

When a teacher asked my name, I said Esther, but he told me it wasn't correct. I was confused. He pronounced it, but I couldn't hear any difference. A few months later, a Chinese immigrant told me that pronouncing 'er' requires the tip of your tongue to curve. But when I said it, I kept my tongue flat.

Here, I met immigrants from different countries, aged twenty to seventy years. I met one classmate who had been in the U.S. for more than thirty years. She told me she had been in this class for a few years, and some immigrants had been here for quite a long time. Many people came here not only for their language but also for social life. As immigrants, they did not have friends and relatives here. In the church, they could meet people and make friends.

The ESL course was fine. The teachers were volunteers who were English speakers, and they had little teaching experience. But they were friendly and nice. I didn't feel very helpful in my English. I ended up with two semesters.

Eight months after I immigrated to the U.S., my Green Card still hadn't arrived. This issue bothered me a lot. I arranged one virtual session with the soul communicator Liqin, who lived next to Shanghai.

Since I started my own business, I built my support systems: I had two to three coaches who were my coaching classmates. Liqin was special. As a soul communicator, she helped me connect with my higher self and uncover emotional blockages at the soul level. I was very open to anything that could support me.

Usually, I shared my issue, and Liqin connected with my soul through the images coming to her mind. Then, she would offer interpretations of the challenges I was facing, often revealing the emotional roots behind them. At the end of each session, she would point out the "soul fragments" or "energy blockages" that needed healing. When she received guidance—such as suggested actions, prayer phrases, or practices to help me connect more deeply with my soul—she would share them with me.

She communicated with my soul and told me I would get my Green Card. She also told me that she had seen a picture of me.

"I see you are in a very beautiful boat that has docked on the lake. The boat has decorations of animals and flowers. You are so fond of this boat, and you caress the boat affectionately. Even though you have your bag and it's time to go, you don't want to leave. You have tears in your eyes."

"Your soul said that boat represented your career in China!"

I was a little shocked, but I knew it was right.

I spent too much time on my career. My business was like my child and it grew up so fast. More and more clients were coming, more and more coaches were joining, and more and more programs were launching. I also released my first book, *Awakening: Design Your Life to Be the Way You Want* (Chinese name 《觉醒: 把人生设计成你想要的样子》) in 2018. Every day, I was working on coaching sessions, training, meetings, and writing articles. I didn't have time to think about the plan in the U.S.

From my point of view, I was still a Chinese entrepreneur and career coach who served Chinese clients after I immigrated. Immigration, for me, just meant changing a place to live. A Green Card represented an immigrant identity and a new role, and I rejected it from my subconscious. Rejecting this new role meant I did not need to worry about fitting into a new culture. I didn't realize I was in the middle of a big life and career transition. I just thought I could continue my Chinese business in the U.S.

Five years later, when I coached immigrant clients from non-English-speaking countries who had business in their birth countries, I mentioned they were in a big career and life transition, and they were shocked. They didn't realize it either.

But they suffered: it was very expensive to live in the U.S. compared to their countries. Their income was reduced. They spent more time in the U.S., which affected their business in their birth countries. On the other side, if they wanted to find a job or do a business that was like what they did in their birth country, it was difficult because of language, culture, certification, and confidence. For a short time, they continued their previous work in their birth country, but they were very anxious about their financial situation.

I had an experience. No matter how much money I made from China, I needed to divide it by seven (exchange rate). For example, my mid-level career coaching case price was nearly 7,000 yuan, and my rent in Shanghai was 6,000 yuan, so I could cover it with one case. But that's only about $1,000 here, while the rent in Charlotte was around $1,600. Back then, I felt it was hard to make money in this way.

Why did I reject this new role? Going deep, I was so scared to let my Chinese career go. This was my identity, my ego. Other career coaches respected me, and some clients even regarded me as a role model. I had a good income, a good social status, and a job that brought me a sense of accomplishment. Although I was so tired, I enjoyed this feeling. Without that, I was nobody in the U.S. This fear held me back.

But my soul was eager for new experiences.

In June 2020, I received my Green Card. I spent nearly one year accepting my new identity—I was an immigrant in the U.S.

with a high education, and I had my own business in my birth country. If I wanted to have my career in the U.S., I needed to do something.

Here, I have professional advice as a career coach for new immigrants or those who are preparing to immigrate to the U.S.

1. Realize that immigration is a big life and career transition; you will lose, and you will gain. You may lose your social status—especially if you held a respected position such as a doctor or professor—as well as the support network of familiar friends and family. You might also miss the ease of enjoying authentic food from your home country, your native language, and the deep cultural connections you grew up with.

In exchange, you may gain a higher quality of life: a modern, spacious home with a yard, two or three cars, and more green space, access to advanced healthcare, cleaner air, a slower pace of life (especially outside big cities), and international career opportunities. You may also experience greater freedom of speech and stronger legal protections for individual rights.

2. Prepare your finances—reasonably save for starting a new degree, skills training, English studying, traveling, and career exploration.

3. Spend some time traveling or living in different places, and then decide where you want to settle down.

4. Give yourself time to adjust to the new life, especially if you have your own business in your birth country. Transition does require time.

5. Build your support system—a life coach, a career coach, a therapist, and additional professional and emotional support from family and friends.

. . .

Losing my Green Card was just the beginning. I didn't realize I was going through a big life and career transition. I was still holding on to my old identity, but life in the U.S. was already pushing me to change. Just as I started to settle in, something unexpected was coming—a global event that would change everything.

Chapter 2
The Pandemic Was on the Way

On December 29th, 2019, I went back to China for our big conference. This was an annual gathering for all the coaches and clients. In the past few years, I had organized our gatherings to meet other coaches and clients.

When I joined in-person events by other organizers, I felt they talked more about business and making money. That bored me. Then, I created my social events—we discussed our self-development and career development. Our attendees were mostly women.

If you don't want to sit at other people's tables, you can host a table by yourself and attract people who have things in common with you. For example, I built my coaching business to help others, especially women. Naturally, I attracted other women who wanted to help women join my team. I hosted my table, and the guests were attracted to the vision we shared.

In 2017, I built an online platform for women's self and career development. We supplied one to two free lessons every month, which attracted more women to join. We had seven WeChat groups with around three thousand women. WeChat is a Chinese social media messaging app.

I found it was a great way to connect with women and help them understand what we did. The most important thing was that we had common values: deep connection, helping others, independence, and self-development.

All the team members, trainees, clients, and potential clients came for this gathering. We had a great time. After that, we had a workshop for all the coaches on how to develop their businesses.

From my experience in training independent coaches, I found that coaches with strong inner strength had an easier time running a successful business. If they experienced too much struggle or self-doubt when confronting new challenges, they often gave up or thought they weren't good enough.

To have strong inner strength, you need to be an independent thinker; you need to know who you are and build your powerful belief systems. So, when I chose coaches to join my team from the pool of trainees, I preferred to choose those kinds of women. I also followed these rules when I chose a business partner.

When I designed our training curriculum system, I gave trainees more time to practice understanding their values, vision, and limiting beliefs. They practiced with their teammates, which helped them build deeper connections. Although they had the online training, they developed deep connections with each other, which made them eager to meet in person.

But I had a tough decision to make. I wanted to take two coaches out of my team. As I said, I need coaches with strong inner strength. The two replaced coaches came from my Advanced Training Program, Cohort 1. That time, I just needed more support, so I quickly selected three coaches, including Tong Zhou, from my first cohort.

I spent a lot of time mentoring them, and I hoped they would grow up fast. Every month, four of us did a case study. But it was difficult to improve in a short time. When the business became bigger, more powerful women joined the training program. I was going to involve two new coaches from my Advanced Training Program, Cohort 3. I had had this idea for a long time.

At first, I was very anxious to run my business—to be fast, to be strong. I needed more hands. I chose three coaches at one time from my first cohort. This was a mistake by an entrepreneur in the first stage. In the beginning, the entrepreneur doesn't have strong leadership skills to lead more team members, as they also need time to grow. Moreover, having more people increased the cost, making expenses higher. The next time, I would remember the balance between quality and quantity.

This is a phase many new entrepreneurs go through in the first stage. We are very anxious for survival and want to grow fast to avoid the fear of failure. The faster the growth, the bigger the goals. During this stage, the ego is exaggerated.

I had a high demand of myself, and I thought I was not good enough. One issue that disturbed me in my life was that I didn't accept and love myself deeply. In Asian culture, parents have high expectations of us, and then we have high expectations of ourselves. The good side is that this encourages us to pursue traditional success—to work hard, be powerful, and make more money or get a prominent position. But when we reach the goal, we are not happy.

Outside, I had a high demand of others. When dissatisfied with them, I simply wanted to replace those people. Small companies are not stable, and employees come and go because the boss's energy goes up and down. The bosses have their own patterns, and ultimately, the bosses prefer to choose people who are similar to themselves. The company culture is cultivated in this way.

The enormous challenge for me was leading people. The relationship with my team members was a tough thing I needed to deal with. There are many issues and complex relationships among women. When we grow up, we don't get more respect and love compared to men. We have many unsatisfied wants and emotions. When a group of women are together, old emotional wounds become entangled in group dynamics. All the drama comes from emotions hidden in the subconscious.

I tried to avoid it; I did not want to spend time on emotions. I wanted to use my logical brain to solve all the problems, though it was not working very well.

In Shenzhen, one of the coaches told me the head coach, Tong Zhou, was not happy. I was confused as to why she was not happy. She had all the support from me, and the other coaches respected her very well. I was told Tong Zhou had emotions about two others being kicked out. She was a classmate of the other two coaches, and they had a good relationship. She also worried that she might be removed in the future.

At that time, my first thought was that if Tong Zhou wanted to quit, I would find a new coach to replace her. It was how I coped with fear and anger, by staying focused on solutions. Rational thinking became my shield. Maybe that was why she didn't feel safe enough to share her true concerns with me.

After meeting some coaches, I explored the good food in Shenzhen, including all kinds of dim sum that I had never seen before, as well as delicious goose stew from Foshan. In the U.S., it is so difficult to eat authentic Chinese food.

After the gathering, I visited my family, who did not live in Shanghai. My second sister asked me when I would have a child. I did not like this topic.

When I was single, my mother also pushed me to get married

early. But I got married when I was thirty-six years old. After I got married, people around me pushed me to have a baby. I did not know whether my mother gave this task to my sister, who liked to play this role. As for Mike's family, they never asked or pushed us, and I felt more spacious.

I told my sister that Mike and I had not decided. For me, I didn't want to have a child. In 2021, we made the final decision not to have a child, and no one disturbed me anymore.

Living in China, you are always pushed to finish your tasks in your lifetime. As a student, you are pushed with homework and studies. When you work, you are pushed to find a boyfriend or girlfriend, buy a house, get married, give birth, and have a second baby. If you are a single woman over thirty years old, you will have more pressure. The horrible thing is that during the Spring Festival, all the family gets together, and all the relatives push you.

I remember when I visited Mike's parents in the UK in the winter. My mother-in-law told me she just listened to the news about the Chinese story at the Spring Festival.

"They pushed their children to find boyfriends or girlfriends, and they always said, 'This is all for your own good.'"

Yes, "This is all for your own good" is their pet phrase. This is how elders force youngsters to do something without taking any responsibility.

My flight back to the U.S. was on January 22nd. I spent my last week in Shanghai at a hotel. I didn't want to bother my classmates, friends, or team members, and it was very convenient to stay at the hotel.

I met one client who had a few virtual sessions when I was in the U.S., and she wanted to meet me in person. My client studied in the U.S. for her bachelor's degree and came back to China when she graduated. She worked at several small companies, but she did not like this life. She mentioned she wanted to go to Germany for a master's degree.

When we met, we discussed Germany and the U.S. She liked the U.S. as she met many strong women, but on the other side, her major, her reading, and her communication with American students let her know more about the dark side of the U.S. In her class, she was the only international student. She liked Germany, which was a combination of socialism and capitalism, and it supported poor people very well.

I shared my experience. I knew the U.S. not only from the book but also from my experience. I had spent one year in the U.S. on the volunteer program. For the first six months, we needed to fundraise to support us to go to Africa, and for the third six months, we needed to find places to show what we had done in Africa.

We drove to different cities, couch-surfed with different people, fundraised from different stores, and met people from different backgrounds. In the U.S., people trust you can make it if you start something, which may be ridiculous in other countries. Also, people are friendly and open. One day, I chatted with a Brazilian team member about fundraising.

"It will be very difficult in China. People think you're lying."

"Also in Brazil!" he laughed.

After she listened to my experience, she said that I was a good fit for the U.S. She was an idealist, and Germany was good for her.

There is no right or wrong choice; it just depends on your values. The clearer you know your values, the easier you can decide. For me, freedom was my core value, and for my client, the equity system was the most important. We followed our own choices. She went to Germany one year later.

I read the book *The Almanack of Naval Ravikant* in 2022.

Naval talks about the three most important choices of our lifetime: 1) What do you do? 2) Where do you live? and 3) Who do you live with? After I made two choices—a job and a partner—I made the choice of place.

Mike wanted to go back to Europe, the UK, France, and even Germany, but he was not very determined. I was very determined to live in the U.S. When we told Mike's parents we would immigrate to the U.S. in 2017, my mother-in-law asked why not the UK. She thought we would like to go to the UK. I was the reason, and the U.S. was always my first choice.

Most of my clients did not spend time on those three important choices, especially on their careers. By the time they reached their forties, many found themselves in managerial roles they didn't enjoy. They didn't like their jobs; they stayed in them for survival and because the pay was good.

At midnight on January 20th, I heard someone scream outside. It woke me up, and I felt terrified. During the daytime, people were very busy and very stressed. At night, some people may use this way to express themselves.

I always felt stressed, and sometimes I couldn't breathe during that week. It looked like something would come. Maybe my body sensed something, but my brain blocked it.

On January 22nd, the last day of the three-week trip, the news about the COVID-19 virus had spread. I learned a little about it from watching YouTube. But I did not watch more. When I went to the dentist, I asked the hygienist to give me extra masks. A few people on the street wore masks.

When I was at Pudong International Airport, a few passengers were waiting for the plane, and almost everyone was wearing masks. When I landed in Dallas on the same day, things were different. It was normal, and it looked like nothing had happened. Scattered people wore masks. I removed my mask, but I felt stressed and scared.

Wuhan's lockdown started at 10:00 a.m. on January 23rd, 2020 (China time), which was 9:00 p.m. on January 22nd in Charlotte. I flew from Dallas at 7:30 p.m. and arrived at Charlotte airport at 10:50 p.m. The lockdown began while I was in the air.

It wasn't until the next day, when I watched a YouTube video, that I found out about the Wuhan's lockdown. I started watching more videos about the virus, and I became more anxious. I told Mike we needed to store some food. He laughed, and I was furious. He didn't believe it would affect the U.S. but I had a feeling it would come.

One night, I even had a dream that I checked myself for COVID-19. In the dream, the test showed me I didn't have it. That day, I went to church for second-semester ESL lessons, and I also went to the Charlotte NPR radio station for a live broadcast with Mike Colin, as I was a donor for NPR that year.

I didn't know that after this trip, I wouldn't be able to travel to China until nearly four years later.

I didn't know this pandemic would change all people's lives on Earth. Looking back, I can now see that I was standing at the edge of a life chapter that was quietly closing—while a new one was already unfolding. The energy had shifted. My body sensed it before my mind caught up. The world was about to pause. And I was about to flow into a new journey.

Chapter 3
The Start of the Pandemic

When Wuhan went on lockdown, the world turned its attention to COVID-19. During the Chinese Spring Festival from January 25th to February 28th, 2020, my Chinese family's WeChat group also shared what happened around there. Some highways between my hometown province and the neighboring province were cut off, and even between small villages, the roads were blocked. Because they controlled people's movements, the virus did not spread quickly in China.

My sister-in-law was pregnant before the pandemic. When she visited her parents in a small village, she could not go back home to the middle-sized city. My brother tried to send her belongings, but he had to stop outside the village because the authorities did not let him in. He left them at the office, and his father-in-law picked them up.

My nephew was born on March 3rd, 2020. He was supposed to be born in May. He was a pandemic baby. I thought he must have felt his mother's and other people's anxiety and sensed the dangers, so he came to this world earlier.

The lockdown in Wuhan trapped one of our trainees, Daniela

Luo. Daniela moved to Canada several years ago, and she brought her daughter to Wuhan to visit her parents for the Spring Festival. She had not celebrated the Chinese Spring Festival with her parents for years. It was such bad luck for her.

We tried to support her emotionally. Daniela gradually became more accepting of the situation. I spent more time watching YouTube videos to learn about COVID-19. The more I watched, the more stressed I felt. But I could not stop, and I got addicted. It felt like an invisible hand was always grabbing me to YouTube.

When the virus became more serious, many countries tried to evacuate their people from Wuhan. At first, Daniela was happy, but she found out she was a Green Card holder and not a Canadian citizen (her husband was Canadian), and she was not eligible to evacuate. The rising hope evaporated. Her situation worried us, and we didn't know when the lockdown would end.

Her luck turned when her husband contacted a Canadian newspaper; her story was published, and many people learned about her situation. Finally, the government agreed to evacuate her and her daughter under pressure from the media.

When she landed for quarantine before they went back home to Canada, we had a video call. She was in a good mood and laughed a lot when she told me the story. I felt happy for her.

We were both born in the 1980s in China; we were often called the post-80s generation. The post-80s generation witnessed China's continuous economic rise, increasing material abundance, and a life marked by safety and stability. We thought we had such a great life. We never imagined we would witness the biggest event in the world. Daniela was a participant. Such a story! When I listened to her, it was just like an Arabian night.

Everyone was scared, but we thought that controlling Wuhan would stop the virus's spread and allow life to return to normal.

I had a memory of SARS in 2003. At that time, I studied at the university. One hospital was next to the east door of our university. All the gates were closed, and if you wanted to go outside of the campus, you had to go north of the door with your ID and fill in the form. People were not allowed to visit the university if they did not work or study here.

We had a big campus, and we had everything. It was okay not to go outside. The authorities planned many kinds of sports competitions. I joined the volleyball team to represent our math department and compete with other teams, and we went to the Top Five.

It was a good memory. We had a lot of fun. A few months later, SARS was controlled, and our lives returned to normal. I thought COVID-19 would be like SARS.

When many Chinese training companies had to cancel their in-person training programs, our online training, which had already been in operation for several years, saw a boost. Our team also worked online, and we had regular meetings every month. After that, they organized their own time. Many companies slowly transferred their services from onsite to offsite. We were fortunate to be at the forefront of online working.

On March 11th, 2020, the World Health Organization (WHO) officially declared COVID-19 a pandemic. On March 13th, President Donald Trump declared a national emergency. On March 19th, California was the first state to issue a stay-at-home order. Other states followed in the days after, including New York, Washington, and Illinois. More and more people got COVID-19. My attention turned back to the U.S.

That day, when I heard an emergency announcement from the government on the radio, I was not so scared. The U.S. was facing an emergency period. It looked like the shoe had finally dropped.

Mike came back from the school and told me that the CMS (Charlotte Mecklenburg School) had closed and that all the teaching would be online. Now he knew it was real. We didn't store more food, but the situation for us was okay. We lived in North Carolina, and there were few cases. Sometimes, Mike could go outside to buy food with a mask.

My client in the UK recommended we use the Instacart app for online food shopping. That way, we didn't even need to go outside. Later, in 2023 and 2024, I coached many software engineers from Instacart.

The authorities in my state gave guidelines about going out only for necessary stuff. For outdoor exercise, you needed to keep a six-foot distance. We rented a house with a big backyard and front yard before the pandemic, so we didn't feel too much difference.

We heard about the pandemic only through the news. All the restaurants were closed, and we could not go indoors (we didn't want to do so), so we explored many outdoor places. We even bought an inflatable kayak. Few people were outside, and it was quiet. It felt so great.

I held a learner's permit, and I practiced driving a car. I couldn't finish my last two driving lessons because of the pandemic. There were no traffic jams on the road.

One day, I drove on the highway at 70 miles per hour, and my heart came to my throat. This was my first time, and I was so nervous. I had to focus on the front. Mike sat next to me, which made me feel a little better. The few cars on the highway also calmed me down a little. After practicing on the highway one to two times, I felt very confident in my high-speed driving skills.

Because of the pandemic, they canceled my road test for my

driver's license. I got my license under a new rule: Mike's signature was enough to confirm my sixty hours of supervised driving. Since he had a license, he was allowed to certify that I had completed the required practice.

I was happy not to have to take an exam. I hated taking any exams after the Gaokao (the national college entrance exam in China). I felt like I had exam-related trauma. After failing the written driving test five times, I prayed to God that I would never have to take another exam.

Finally, God helped me.

My mother-in-law said that in her lifetime, she had only known two people who didn't need to take an exam to get a driver's license. One was her father, who was a police officer in the UK. One was me. In that case, I thanked the pandemic.

The pandemic halted our busy lives, like pressing a pause button. We had more time to stay at home. We adopted two kittens who were siblings. We named the male kitten Freedom, which is my core value, and the female kitten Hope. We hoped we could still see hope even if we were experiencing a pandemic.

The most inconvenient part of the pandemic was that we could not get haircuts. Hair salons were closed. We tried to cut each other's hair with scissors. It was quite fun and easier than I thought. The most difficult side was the back. I didn't know how to cut different layers, and Mike's hair looked like a dog bite. Luckily, we just needed to show our front sides for online meetings, and no one could see the back of our heads except for each other. We could not meet acquaintances; it was totally fine to have messed-up hair.

When I volunteered in Malawi, my teammate, a Korean girl, Yujin, cut my hair, and it was a great haircut. She said when she studied in Japan, the haircuts were expensive, so she learned to cut hair. Many overseas students cut each other's hair. I thought she was so smart and that I could never do it.

The pandemic made me learn a new skill. With more practice, I got better. Cutting each other's hair made Mike and me closer. We were like an old couple taking care of each other.

Every day, I checked the number of COVID-19 cases in *The New York Times*. It snowballed. On April 28th, 2020, the U.S. surpassed one million confirmed COVID-19 cases. When I called my mother, she checked on me and Mike first, then said,

"Your country—the U.S.—is in such terrible shape. One million people have gotten COVID-19!"

From her words, it sounded like there were dead bodies on the streets of the U.S. But I did not know anyone who had died from COVID-19. I did not sense it.

My mother was born in the 1940s. She was a Red Guard during the Cultural Revolution. The Cultural Revolution was a political movement in China from 1966 to 1976, led by Mao Zedong. Its goal was to remove old traditions and ideas, but it caused chaos—many people were punished, schools were closed, and cultural items were destroyed.

The Red Guards were groups of young people who followed Mao Zedong during the Cultural Revolution. They aimed to remove old traditions, attack intellectuals, and support communist ideals. Many Red Guards took part in violent actions and caused great social and cultural damage.

My mother said she had never taken part in any violent actions. But I found she was very good at playing the friend-or-enemy game. In her mind, she put me in the position of representative of the U.S., and she was representing China.

When I talked to some classmates, I noticed a similar black-or-white mindset. For example, one classmate brought up what she had seen on Chinese social media about the origin of the virus. Her view was that it must have come from either China or the U.S.—these were the only two options. Her answer was "from the U.S." When she talked about it, she became very emotional. At that point, the conversation usually could not last longer.

Later, I learned this type of thinking is called "all-or-nothing thinking." It overlooks complexity and nuance, leading to rigid, oversimplified judgments, which bring anxiety and conflict to the conversation.

It was the price to pay for being an immigrant. We lived in different cultures and political systems and used different ways to gain information compared to our original family and previous friends. A good way to keep the peace for me was less communication and not talking about politics and the differences between the two countries.

Later, Mike and I received Economic Impact Payments. The first Economic Impact Payment was $1,200, the second Economic Impact Payment was $600, and the third one was $1,400 in 2021. This was my first time getting money from the government, and it was a totally new experience for me. I even forgot to tell my mother this information as maybe I did not want her to know I had money in my pocket.

I felt lucky to have more space at home, a spacious backyard, and access to nature, while many people had to stay inside high-rise apartments. But I never imagined the pandemic would hit me in such an unexpected way.

Chapter 4
The Loss of Two Business Partners

I n my work, I felt more suffering.

Following the dismissal of two coaches in April, one month after the pandemic, Tong Zhou told me she wanted to quit. I was still shocked when it happened. I tried my best to keep her and told her she could do whatever she wanted to do. She agreed.

But a few days later, she came to me and showed more emotion. I spent a lot of time soothing her. After every conversation, I felt emotionally drained and frustrated. Her negative emotions affected me, and I could not digest them.

In this relationship, I found that I was like her boyfriend. I took care of her, including her emotions. When I moved to the U.S., another coach, Yali Yu, took charge of daily operations; she was more rational and seemed like a friend. We had a brotherhood, despite both being women—she was strong, loyal, and gave me more support.

At first, I was very close to Tong Zhou, but I was not able to take all the emotion from her. Then, I got close to Yali. I could feel Tong Zhou was angry with me because Yali and I were closer. I released a little anger from Tong Zhou when I got close to Yali.

Through a few exhausting conversations, I agreed with Tong Zhou that she should quit. I was exhausted. I felt like I had nothing left to give. I told her she didn't need to be on our team and that she could just be one of our trainers. When we had the training program, she could come to give her lessons. Then, she would have more time to build her business and her brand. She said this was okay.

However, two weeks after Tong Zhou quit our team, she started her training program ahead of our Advanced Training Program, and some clients from our Basic Training Program followed her. I was angry and hurt. I could not believe she had done this. She was not a person who liked to make money.

I had a dream: guns shot me in open land, and there was no place to hide. It felt like my subconscious was showing me just how defenseless and vulnerable I had become through this experience. I always tried to help women and never wanted to argue and fight with them, but I got betrayed by the woman I trusted fully.

I shared my dream with Tong Zhou, and she felt sorry. She insisted that she had not meant to do that. We both had very low energy. I told her we could not cooperate in the future, and we ended our partnership.

We broke up!

I told Mike that I didn't want to continue my Chinese business. Mike said,

"Then give up, and you will have more opportunities in the U.S."

But how did I give up what I created? I could not do it, and I felt trapped. I knew that I had to let this thought go.

I had to continue, as I had six team members, including three new members. Usually, we had a self-development meeting every three months to share our personal development, and other coaches could comment. I was very open and wrote a lot before we started. When other coaches saw I was openhearted, they also shared deep things. Those meetings were our favorite—we felt deeply connected through expressing our true ideas and listening to others.

In one meeting, I shared my feelings about Tong Zhou, and the other coaches gave me feedback:

"You were in the game of friendship, only with two people," one coach said.

"From my observation at the conference in Shenzhen in January, it looked like, in your eyes, there was only Tong Zhou. You couldn't see other people. In Tong Zhou's eyes, there was only you. No one could get between you. One day, when a third person came into this relationship, the balance was broken."

Another coach said:

"Yes, it looked like Tong Zhou always wanted to get your attention. But she did not know it was impossible. More people will come to you, and you cannot always focus on her. When you turned attention to other people, she felt she was abandoned. In her opinion, you are a scumbag who likes the new and loathes the old."

A word awakens the dreamer.

Yes, I always played the two-person relationship game. It originated in my relationship with my mother. She treated me the best compared to other siblings, and I treated her as the closest person. During my time in school, I was always looking for a best friend.

But my relationship with Tong Zhou was different. I could not absorb her emotions, and I wanted to leave. She was like my mother, who had more negative emotions than positive. My mother shared all her negative emotions with me, and I sometimes played her husband's role when I was young.

29

Usually, I used two ways to protect myself. The first one was to be rational. Sometimes, I was very calm when listening to my mother's story. I found several of my female clients had similar situations with their mothers: emotional mothers and rational daughters.

When I traveled to Alaska, I met a mother and her daughter in a restroom at Ted Stevens Anchorage International Airport. The mother was busy on her phone. She was crying while she was talking to someone and was trying to get tissues for her tears and snot. It seemed she was talking to a woman. A little daughter washed her hands by herself. When the mother said something on the phone, the little girl replied:

"I am happy to be with you."

She was so rational, and I did not feel she was happy or sad. With her emotional mother, the little girl looked like an adult. I was like her when I was young.

My second way was to escape from my mother whenever I could do it. My high school studies made it possible, as I had to live at the school. When I graduated from the university, I went to Beijing, hundreds of miles from my mother. Like my relationship with my mother, on one side, I liked Tong Zhou, and on the other side, I wanted to keep away from her.

I understood why Tong Zhou was angry enough to try to get revenge. It looked like I had abandoned her.

I found that when groups of women were together, some women projected onto others as having different roles: some like the mother, some like the father, some like the older sister, some like the younger sister, and some like friends.

Also, we had the psychology of gender in our minds. In terms of my psychological gender, I was a man. My mission was to support vulnerable women. I asked this question to other coaches on our team, and only Lei Guo, who had long hair, said she had the psychological gender of a woman. Five female coaches—me, Yali, Xin Zhao, Xiaoyun Li, and Jing Wang—had the psychological gender of a man, and we all had short hair. When we met, we became a family.

I didn't know whether I needed to talk to Tong Zhou to explain everything. One day, when we were having a meeting, Xin Zhao said, "If you love someone, the best way is to let this person experience on his own!"

Immediately, I knew my answer from my heart: I would give both of us the time to have our own experiences.

But I hadn't had a chance to rest after Tong Zhou's event—other issues drained my energy.

We had a trainer, Ting Liu, who was not part of my team. I knew her from a training in Shanghai after I came back from my volunteer program. She was a brave woman, and she started her career coaching business after she got career coaching training. She wrote brief articles to attract clients to her official WeChat account.

Inspired by her, I did my private practice with my official WeChat account. I enjoyed writing the articles, and I wrote many case studies, which attracted more clients. I found that I had written one article that attracted two to three clients. It was my business booster. More and more clients came to me. Ting Liu and I were always keeping in touch.

One day, she suggested that I start my mentoring program for career coaches. I had practiced for a long time, and she was new and needed mentoring. Following her suggestion, I started this Advanced Training Program. In Cohort 1, she served as both trainee and trainer. She had worked as a salesperson for a long time, so I let her train in sales skills and social media marketing. We cooperated very well.

Not long after, she got pregnant and gave birth to her baby. I witnessed her becoming a mother during our partnership. After she gave birth, she developed her training lesson in a way that was similar to her work with our trainees. For the Basic Training Program, she also mentioned her own training. Training assistants told me about this a few times. I was angry about her behavior. I tried to warn her on WeChat, and she was angry about my warning.

Later, she told me that if I wanted her to be the trainer for the Advanced Training Program, she would bring her own assistant with the program. She did not want to use our training assistant. When I shared this request with the team, they thought it did not follow the rules.

That night, after my conversation with her, I had a dream. I saw a turtle's egg being taken away from its body. The turtle died. My subconscious let me know I could not cooperate with her anymore.

When we had a last conversation, I told her my decision, and she ended the video call, forcing the conversation to end. But we had little emotional entanglement. We were both rational, and we ended our relationship rationally. No fight, no argument.

The events with Tong Zhou and Ting Liu happened one after the other. For the Advanced Training Program, I had to push my new team members to be the trainers. I did not have a backup. One of the trainers, Hanbing Huang, discussed with me that I had better sign a contract with the other trainers in the future. The trainer could not take the trainees to their own training program. I also needed to apply for copyright protection for my course.

When I felt hurt by other coaches, I received even more support from Hanbing. Hanbing was my first client when I started my business in 2016. She flew from a provincial capital city in the south of China to Shanghai for her career transition coaching session. At the time, her baby was ten months old, and she brought her husband and her son to Shanghai.

After the sessions, she changed jobs from civil engineering to career counseling, focusing on high school students. In China, students choose their majors, and universities have had more freedom since the Gaokao reform. This was an enormous opportunity for career counseling. Many people jumped into this industry.

Hanbing built her company and found a business partner through me. I wrote about her case in my first book, and my mother read her story and always said with her thumb up,

"Hanbing is so great!"

My mother raised six children, and she had to quit her teaching job when she had her sixth child. She respected Hanbing's courage.

While Hanbing was pregnant with her second child, she was busy developing her business. I witnessed her growth process as well. From her, I saw a Chinese woman working hard to pursue her career. Chinese women work responsibly and devotedly to support their families and careers.

One of my business strategies was to choose strong clients to cooperate with. I invited Hanbing to teach the coaching in her area, and we both benefited from our cooperation.

I felt very lucky to have her by my side.

I was so tired, and every day while cooking, my brain wouldn't stop; business problems and solutions consumed my every thought, leaving me exhausted. My thoughts controlled me.

When others experienced the loss of loved ones, lives, or jobs in the early stage of the pandemic, I went through the loss of two business partners.

Why did this situation happen during the pandemic? I had my answers later. If we regarded the Earth as a person, the pandemic was a disaster. When the person became sick, the energy was low. We were in a low-energy state, which triggered negative emotions. Tong Zhou, Ting Liu, and I were hooked on the negative energy of the environment.

It was so painful! I never knew we had come to this stage. I thought we could cooperate for a long time. We had a lot of fun in our WeChat group, sharing how to deal with different clients. Then we ended up this way. I was exhausted.

When I attended a coaching training about energy, I saw a picture with a somatic reaction to emotions. I liked the person who was happy. The energy through their bodies was red and yellow. For negative emotions, the body was full of dark colors.

I imagined one day I would have yellow and red happiness energy. I didn't need to be rich or successful; I just wanted to be that kind of person with radiant energy. Even if I met a stranger on the street who was not happy or treated me badly, I could still feel happy. This was the person I wanted to be. Joyful and peaceful, unconditionally.

That incident during the pandemic hit me hard—it woke me up from my constant chase for worldly success and made me realize there were deeper lessons I needed to learn in life.

Only pain that deep could spark a real desire to change. Even my body would have a reaction to this pain!

Chapter 5
A Painful Arm

When I was overwhelmed by the turmoil in my business, my body added to the chaos—as they say, when it rains, it pours. The pain in my right arm had grown significantly worse to the point where I could barely lift it.

This pain first started back in June 2018, when I launched the Nan Ding program, a one-year online course focused on self-development and career development for women. I tried acupuncture, electromagnetic therapy, and massage in Shanghai. I went to the hospital every week. But it only helped a little.

One night after I came to the U.S., I had a dream: a hand held my neck and tried to kill me. The nightmare awakened me. I realized this dream wanted to tell me my arm's pain was more serious.

I found a new massage therapist in Charlotte, and it didn't work very well. I went to yoga and swimming; the pain was still getting worse, and I could not use my right arm to do normal work like writing and cutting food. I had to train my left hand to work. I was so confused as it came all of a sudden, and I didn't know why.

My body was so exhausted, and in my heart, I really wanted to start my American career. In 2018, when I coached my clients in

Shanghai, a thought came to me: I would coach clients from different backgrounds in the U.S., which made me very excited. Now, I was in the U.S., but my Chinese business trapped me. What happened to me was so painful and made me feel hopeless.

I asked Yali to handle daily business operations and team management. Then, I could move my attention to starting my American business, but she said she could not do it on her own.

I chose Yali as the manager to organize most things, but for the marketing and coaching training, she did not have much experience. However, her human resource management experience and attention to detail were both strong. She organized most things and communicated with me, and I trusted her.

She was rational and very curious. During our self-development meeting, we gave her feedback that she was eager to learn new things, like an enthusiastic boy. But her energy didn't flow easily. It felt too rigid and overly stable. The more flowing your energy is, the stronger you become. For our team, she was like a mother to us and took care of everything.

She asked me to bring another coach, Xin Zhao, so the two of them could take the weight off my shoulders. Xin Zhao was my client. Then, she attended the training, and I invited her to join my team.

She had been a journalist for a decade in a capital city in southeastern China. She read more than most people, and she brought more spiritual knowledge to our team, as well as my life. She was wise and could see things deeply. And she knew how to cooperate with the authorities at any stage in her life. She worked at a government newspaper, which gave her excellent skills in dealing with complex relationships. She shared insights from a high-level perspective. She was a very strong woman. I read more books from her recommendation, and I cultivated a more holistic view.

I talked to her, and she agreed with it. I paid the two of them to handle the things that I handled. The cost increased. Money was not a problem, and what I needed was to take a rest.

I was burnt out.

To my surprise, a few weeks after this decision, my arm recovered, and I was no longer in pain.

I knew this pain was connected to my subconscious. Back in 2016, I read a book called *Your Body Knows the Answer* by Chinese psychologist Zhihong Wu. It explores the connection between body and mind—and how our subconscious can express itself through the body.

In February 2017, after a beautiful three-week trip to the UK with Mike, which was my first time visiting his family, I returned to Shanghai. I rested for only two days before jumping back into work. Soon after, I developed a persistent cough. It got so bad that I couldn't lie down at night, and I had to sleep sitting up, leaning against the headboard. I saw a doctor and took medicine, but it helped little. It took about two weeks to fully recover.

After I recovered, I realized how much I had enjoyed that trip: delicious food, warm family connections, a good time with fun entertainment activities, and cozy moments sitting by the fireplace. But the moment I returned, my body was thrown from a relaxed state into high stress—dealing with anxious clients, managing social media, and more. That sudden shift triggered my body to send a clear message: slow down. But my mind was racing. I was anxious to get back to work, and it took time for my awareness to catch up.

That experience was the beginning of paying attention to my body. Still, years later, when I experienced arm pain, I didn't yet understand what my subconscious was trying to tell me. I knew I had to keep exploring.

I bought more books that talked about the relationship between illness and the subconscious. I found answers in a book called *Spontaneously Healed: A Complete Guide to Holistic Mind–Body–Spirit Health* (Chinese name 《不药而愈: 身心灵整体健康完全讲义》) by Yiren Wang from Taiwan.

Doctor Wang explains how illness develops:

First, we have the belief in binary opposition. We label things such as good or bad, strong or weak, which originate from our ego. Then we deny and struggle with the label, and we have conflicts. Prolonged inner conflicts reduce our energy field and fill us with negative energy, such as anger, fear, etc.

Eventually, negative energy affects the body, and symptoms begin to appear—sometimes after days or even weeks. That is why when we do not feel good and go to the hospital for an exam, everything about our biochemistry looks fine.

Doctor Wang also lists the connection between different illnesses and different limiting beliefs. I read about shoulder and arm pain. Wang explains that I "carry too much of other people's responsibility." I realized I had a limiting belief. I was a strong woman, and other women were weak. I needed to carry them, and this was my responsibility.

When I was young, I was outstanding. I was the only child of my generation in my family to go to university. Now, I had my own business. Most clients came to me because they thought I was strong. I carried women on my shoulders—clients, team members, trainees. When I started the Nan Ding program, there were 220 ordinary women who were weak in my mind. I put them all on my shoulders. That was the reason my arm was in pain.

This limiting belief originally came from my ego: I was strong, and I was unique. Other women were weak, and I needed to strengthen my ego by supporting weak women. This was the game my ego liked to play.

When I took most of the burden from my shoulders to Yali and Xin Zhao, I felt relieved. This chronic pain had lasted for over two years. My recovery taught me more about connecting with my body. When I listened consistently and patiently, I always found answers within.

I found many rational and strong women had these limiting beliefs. Some women were the first children in their families and put siblings and parents on their shoulders. Some were the executives and carried all the team members on their shoulders.

Doctor Wang shares many methods for healing the body, but I found two mantras especially helpful and easy to use. For example, if you have belly pain, you can say:

"Dear belly, thank you—you are the best, and I truly love you."

The other mantra is:

"Dear belly, I'm sorry. My conflicting thoughts and beliefs caused your pain. But I am working on transforming myself, and I sincerely ask for your forgiveness."

You can replace "belly" with any part of your body and repeat these mantras for a few minutes every day.

Later, one coach recommended to me an English book, *You Can Heal Your Life,* by Louise Hay, which offers a similar idea.

When I coached American clients, I noticed that many of them faced similar struggles.

One client—a white woman in her twenties—had only worked for a year before being forced to stay home because of body pain and muscle weakness. She was trying to find remote work online. From a young age, she had carried the emotional weight of her family, especially after her parents divorced. She took on the role of caretaker of her siblings. When we talked about her body, she admitted she was angry with her body. So much emotion was stored inside, with no outlet. I recommended some books to help her process her pain.

Another client, an African American woman in her early thirties, suffered from back and chest pain and couldn't work outside the home. She still lived with her parents.

In one session, I asked her what she wanted in the next year. She shared her vision: growing her business, getting more contracts, buying a new car, moving into her own place, and starting a family. When she finished, we both laughed—realizing it was a lot to expect in one year. Then she said,

"I hate my body—it's holding me back from getting what I want."

Women at their age should be creating, exploring, and moving forward. But chronic illness had paused their journey. I believe their bodies were sending important messages—urging them to stop and listen. I hope one day they'll turn inward, reconnect with their bodies, and find the answers they're looking for.

I used to think helping others meant carrying them on my shoulders and doing things for them. But this experience helped me cultivate a new way: to give time and energy to myself first, to live fully as a peaceful and joyful person.

From that place, I can naturally share good energy—with others, with my surroundings, and even with the Earth. When my coaching clients come to me, they can feel the calm energy I bring. When people read my book, they can sense the peace in the words. Even when I meet a dog or cat, they come closer and let me pet them. This joyful energy flows from me and gently touches everything around me.

This painful journey with my arm became more than just a physical challenge. It was my body's way of asking me to stop, listen, and let go. As I slowly reconnected with my body and shifted the beliefs rooted deep in my subconscious, I realized I needed more support to truly care for myself and nurture my joyful energy. And soon, that support appeared: my new coach entered my life.

Chapter 6
My New Coach

I joined ICF Charlotte as a member in June, three months after the pandemic began. The International Coaching Federation (ICF) is a global organization that sets professional standards, provides certification, and supports the advancement of coaching worldwide.

I attended one virtual session about how to help people who had suffered from the pandemic. That's where I met Hellen Yang, a Chinese Canadian coach who would later become a Master Certified Coach (MCC) by ICF in 2023. She coaches, mentors, and trains coaches and leaders to become their best selves and better support their clients and teams through the power of coaching.

I was inspired and felt connected to her good energy. During our one-on-one Zoom meeting, she showed me how to work with my negative emotions instead of rejecting them. I made her my new coach. My previous Chinese coaches didn't have great energy, and they could not support me very well. I had been thinking about finding a new coach for a few months, and then Hellen came into my life.

When I chose the people to support me, I usually focused on the energy of the person. I read the book *Power Vs. Force* by David R. Hawkins in 2019 and learned the importance of energy.

This book introduces a scale of consciousness that measures different emotional and energetic states. At the lowest end is shame, which has an energy level of 20, while at the highest is enlightenment, ranging from 700 to 1000.

One key level is courage, rated at 200—this is the turning point. Once someone reaches the courage level, they move from fear-based energy to empowering energy. Success becomes more accessible—not because of what they're doing, but because of the energy they're doing it with.

I practiced the Hawkins Scale in my life and work. I found that people with high energy were more likely to attract others. Most of the time, my energy could be at a courage level. But my energy was not stable. Sometimes, I bounced around with fear and anger. I was angry because women were not treated very well. This angry energy pushed me to support women through my business.

From my experience, I also observed that energy played an important role in coaching and counseling. Many of my clients told me I had high energy. But burnout took more energy out of me, and I could feel my energy becoming stagnant. I needed flowing and joyful energy to help me unblock myself.

Hellen had very pure and flowing energy, and she was a good fit for me.

All our coaching sessions were conducted virtually. Hellen's Chinese was rusty at the time, as she hadn't spoken it in her everyday life since moving to Vancouver, Canada over twenty years ago. I was surprised that she could forget her native language, but then I realized if I didn't speak Chinese regularly, I might forget words too. During our sessions, I had to speak

English. Sometimes when I couldn't find the right English words, I used Chinese instead. I didn't know if she fully understood, but somehow, our sessions always went smoothly.

She helped me embrace my emotions, and in nearly every session, I cried. I had a pattern of working hard. I thought that if I worked hard, I would deserve what I had. This working hard came from my ancient DNA. For thousands of years, China was a farming country. People had to work hard with their hands just to survive. Farmers followed the seasons—waking up early and working all day, especially during planting and harvest time.

There's an old belief in China: "Hard work brings prosperity." It became part of our culture, especially because of Confucian values.

When I was young, I saw this in my mother. As a stay-at-home mom, she started doing chores right after waking up and didn't stop until she went to bed. She didn't have weekends or holidays. She worked more than twelve hours every day.

Working hard helped me to grow my business, but I felt so tired and stressed.

Also, I saw I treated myself so badly during sessions. I always thought I was not good enough. I didn't give myself good self-care. I set a new goal, and when I finished a goal, I did not feel very happy, and I just moved on to pursue the next one. I needed to prove I was good by reaching more goals. If I couldn't reach them, it meant I was not good enough. I pushed myself so hard that I developed chronic pain, especially in my shoulders and back.

In one coaching session, I felt my shoulder pain flare up. Hellen invited me to listen to what my shoulders were trying to tell me. I took a moment to connect with my shoulders, and I could hear the message they were sending me. Then, I went to the kitchen and got a towel with hot water to put on my shoulders. I really felt that I cared about my shoulders. I cried a lot for myself and for my shoulders.

I learned from Hellen by taking a moment to listen and connect with parts of my body that required my attention. It was a great way to care for and connect with different parts of my body.

I remember one session that helped me understand why I started my business. I had a clear picture. I walked into a dark tunnel alone. People outside wanted to talk to me, but I could not hear them. I focused on my journey. This tunnel had weak light from the far end. I was scared and lonely, and I put my arms across my body as I walked. I knew I had to cross this tunnel. This was my journey. I needed to be with myself.

Finally, I reached the end of the tunnel. Outside the tunnel, there were beautiful wildflowers, trees, sunlight, and trails. I walked along the small trail to feel nature. Then, I took a compact car to the beach. In the sea, I swam and rested. After that, I didn't know where I needed to go.

I realized that from 2016 to 2019 in Shanghai, I had come to this stage that I had created. Most of the time, I stayed alone—I worked at home with no coworkers. Every day, I saw my husband and the delivery men. I didn't want to connect with friends, classmates from school, or ex-coworkers in Shanghai.

When I had a team, one of my team members said she felt I closed my heart, kept other people outside, and felt very distant. Yes, it looked like they tried to talk to me outside the tunnel, but I could not hear. I closed myself in to let myself connect with myself and experience fear and loneliness before I rejected it. In that case, I did not have enough energy to open my heart to the outside. During my business, I felt very stressed. But I appreciate what I experienced.

In another coaching session, Hellen invited me to choose

someone who had supported me. After I named the person, she raised her right hand through our Zoom screen and said,

"Imagine this hand represents the person who has supported you. Where would you like to feel this support—on your shoulder, back, or elsewhere?"

After I identified the part of my body that needed the support, she would gently place her hand there virtually. It was magical. I could really feel her supporting hand on my shoulder and back as I imagined it.

After that, I said something in response to the support, and Hellen would repeat what I said. When I fully immersed myself in this practice, I realized that many women had been supporting me all along, but I didn't see it. I used to see myself only working alone, carrying everything and everyone by myself. But actually, I was able to grow my business because of the help and support from my team, clients, family, friends, and many other women.

When I was busy and stressed, my mind became narrow, and I couldn't see the support that was already around me. I really appreciated other people's support. Without them, I would not have come this far. In my narrow thinking, I believed I was here only because I worked hard, that I was brave and strong. But when I look back on this journey, I can see clearly that I made it through because of the surrounding support.

I later learned from Hellen that this approach was part of her training in somatic coaching.

Over five years, Hellen has supported me through all my transitions. We've had about seventy sessions. Hellen was very creative and flexible. She combined different methods and adapted them to my situation to help me create awareness during our coaching sessions.

Through her coaching, I realized that coaching isn't just about asking questions—it's about guiding clients to create inner experiences that lead to new awareness.

During some sessions, I cried for ten or twenty minutes. She held that space for me. She also helped me create space between myself and my body so I could better care for it. In one session, after expressing a lot of emotion, I told her I needed to rest. She gave me that space. I drank water, then lay down on my mat, and we continued our session from there.

I am a visual person—I love to create with my imagination. I wasn't born this way, but I trained my brain to do it. These visualizations helped me build many future pictures and new self-images: Titan Arum, Maleficent, a black panther, Coraline, a white horse, a blue whale, the Kenai River in Alaska, a slow British train running along the coast, a white bald eagle.

One session revealed my masculine strength—my desire to fight, to be aggressive and ambitious. I had always rejected that part of myself. In the session, I saw a male black panther trapped in a cage in my heart. It growled in its cage, pacing back and forth, then fiercely slammed its paws against the iron bars. It wanted out. I had locked it up because I feared it would hurt others.

But eventually, I opened the cage. It ran onto the African grasslands. It hunted, fought, endured storms, healed itself, found a mate, raised cubs, grew old, and finally died alone at sunrise. It lived a full life—as a male black panther.

Hellen followed her intuition about what was needed in that moment and asked me if I was open and willing to go outside of my house and run for a bit. I accepted her intuitive request, went outside, and ran for ten minutes. I noticed that all the pressure I was feeling earlier had left my body through my breath during running.

I also realized that masculine energy is part of me. Everyone has both masculine and feminine energy. I didn't need to reject it —it helped me take risks, fight for what mattered, and pursue what I wanted.

After that session, I felt at peace.

In another session, I had tension and stiffness from my neck down to the middle of my spine, including both shoulders, after working on many clients. It felt terrible. I lay on the sofa and saw myself as a soldier on a horse, wearing heavy armor. The armor kept my body upright, so I couldn't rest. Hellen asked,

"What color is your horse?"

That question stunned me. I had never paid attention to the horse. It was just a tool for battle. I turned my head to look—and saw a gorgeous white horse. I felt she was tired, too.

I got off her back and removed her saddle, halter, bridle, and reins. Then, the relationship changed. I became a Liberty Trainer, like in the Canadian TV drama *Heartland,* which was about a family who ran a horse ranch, focusing on healing horses and navigating life's ups and downs with love and resilience.

When I raised my hands, my horse lifted her front legs, stood on her hind legs, and danced. When I lowered my body, she gently lay down on the ground. This training uses body language, voice, and emotional connection to work with the horse—no physical restraints.

Finally, I let her go. She ran to the mountains to live with wild horses. Sometimes, she visited me and brought me to beautiful places for sunset. Each time she ran to me, her shining mane flowing in the light; she was full of joy and pure energy.

My relationship with myself has completely transformed. I used to treat myself like a tool to survive life, driven by fear. Now, I was learning to connect with my spiritual self and allow the joyful part of me to come through.

This coaching session helped me shift my self-image from a

soldier to a free white horse. My life energy transformed from fear to joy. In the following months, I continued doing deep inner work, and to my surprise, the stiffness and tension that had bothered me for years disappeared—and never returned. I healed myself.

As a coach, I know it's not the coach who heals the client—it's the client who heals themselves. With positive energy, presence, and powerful questions, coaches help clients connect with their inner resources and see themselves from new angles.

The coach–coachee relationship is truly reciprocal. When I became an international coach, our work together also inspired Hellen to reconnect with her Chinese roots. She devoted herself to relearning her mother tongue, and soon regained her once-lost language. As a result, she took a leap when the opportunity came and co-founded a five-hundred-member coaching community in China, helping ensure Chinese-speaking coaches have access to advanced coaching, mentorship and credentialing.

Every coaching session helped me go deeper and reconnect with myself. I experienced a gradual inner transformation. The stagnant energy within me slowly became clearer and began to flow.

I could feel the energy inside like a small creek gently carrying away the long-settled mud and tiny stones from its bed. The flowing water slowly cleaned the channel, making it smoother and more open. When inner change flows with ease, outer change follows naturally—it's only a matter of time.

Chapter 7
Pausing the Business

On February 8th, 2021, eleven months after the pandemic began, Mike and I went to Sugar Ski Mountain for skiing. We rented a cabin on a farm for three nights, and every morning, we drove to a ski resort.

When we rented all the equipment on the first day, we did not know where we needed to start. We saw a lift crowded with people. We followed them and took the lift. The lift went higher and higher, and we saw beautiful sights. Then I found this lift went to the top of the hill—the most difficult slope. My goodness.

When the lift stopped, we tried to get off, but we both fell on the slope, and the staff had to stop the lift. We stood up and told him we had come to the wrong lift. We didn't even know how to ski, so he sent us back.

Mike took a lesson, and I practiced on the easiest slope. I went skiing once when I lived in Beijing and had a little experience. On the second day, I went to the blue one, which was a little difficult slope.

Many people were taking the lift, and I had the chance to share it with different people. Some were young kids, boys and girls. I couldn't believe they could ski at such a young age. I met a boy who was very extroverted and even started the conversation with me. His parents brought him and his younger brother sking. They took a lift with his brother, and he had to take a lift with other people. He looked like a little man. I also met a woman who could surf very well and was curious about snow-boarding. She hoped her surfing skills could help her learn to snowboard more easily. I was so inspired by their stories.

I tried to control my speed when the slope was very steep, as I was so scared. Sometimes, I had to fall to avoid going too fast. I had my mantra all the time:

"Esther is safe, Esther is focused, Esther is relaxed."

When I connected with my body very well, I could enjoy high speed sometimes. I focused on my left foot and right foot. It was great to enjoy the high speed, even with fear.

When we went back to the cabin, we made food, and I did yoga and read my other long mantra:

"I am the power and presence of God creating this. It's not real. It's completely made up. It is just a story, a creation of my consciousness. It is true joy in disguise. I reclaim my power from this creation now. I feel this power running through my body. When I feel this surge, I feel that I am more and more powerful, and I am getting closer to my true self, showing more of my true self in my life experience. I am feeling myself open to infinite power.

Esther is relaxed, Esther is cheerful, Esther is prosperous, Esther is love.

Esther is truth, Esther is kindness, Esther is beauty, Esther is light.

Esther is happy, Esther is healthy, Esther is peaceful, Esther is joyful.

Esther is free, Esther is open, Esther is compassionate, Esther is enlightened."

When I read "I am feeling myself open to infinite power," I opened my two arms on top of my head and looked up at the universe. I felt the energy come through my whole body.

This mantra is from the book *Busting Loose from the Business Game* by Robert Scheinfeld. Xin Zhao shared it with us. It was very practical, and I had practiced it nearly every day.

I benefited from many mantras. I even wrote my own mantras, learning from my team members. As negative voices echoed in my brain every second, the mantras helped me get rid of those voices and change them into positive energy. Especially when I read them loudly, I felt more positive.

Words had power.

For the two days, I felt very brave. My skiing skills had improved by leaps and bounds. I opened my body, and my heart let me go. I just followed my body. I was not afraid of falling.

When I connected with and trusted my body, it led me to enjoy the thrill of high speed while skiing downhill—something I never thought I could do. My mind had always told me it was dangerous, and I used to waste so much energy trying to control the speed that I couldn't enjoy the experience. But this time, it was a great experience to truly embrace the speed and have fun.

I did not take any skiing lessons. Usually, I watched skiing videos on YouTube, then closed my eyes to imagine that I was skiing like the people in the video. I began practicing skiing from there. I repeated this process until I had mastered skiing. I used visualization to learn new skills, such as swimming, and it worked very well. This was a cheap and effective way to self-study.

When we drove back, we stopped at an old grocery store that

has over one hundred years of history. I went to the back of the store, where there was a creek. I sat next to the creek and watched the water. I didn't want to go back to sit in my room to do Chinese work.

"I want to stop my Chinese business."

When I talked to Mike, I was so surprised. But my brain told me:

"You can't do that. That is all you have!"

Also, I heard another voice from my heart and my legs,

"Let it go!"

Yes, let it go.

From skiing, I conquered my fear, and I wanted to take a brave step.

I asked for a meeting with Yali and Xin Zhao. I shared my thoughts that I was going to pause all the training programs and just continue with individual coaching. Through our discussion, we decided to finish all the ongoing programs and not start any new ones.

Xin Zhao was preparing for the updated Nan Ding program. She said she was very happy to stop. They both felt very tired, especially during the pandemic, and clients and trainees took a lot of energy from them. I had this feeling.

Then, we had a team meeting. During our meeting, Jing Wang was late, and she said she had overslept. From her subconscious, perhaps she didn't want to have this meeting. She had just started her private practice, and she wanted more company.

But the team agreed with the pause: we would all rest until 2023. During those two years, everyone could focus on their own brands.

It was time for our Advanced Training Program, Cohort 4's

ending ceremony, and as I announced this news, they were very shocked. One trainee said,

"We may be the last trainees for the independent career coaches' training program." (She was right, for now.)

From 2019 to 2021, I finally let myself pause. I knew inside that I always had a voice to start a new life. But with the old life in China, it was difficult to start a new one in the U.S. I spent a long time seeing my desire and getting the courage to make this move. The pandemic was one reason. The outer world was a kind of pause, which gave me time to think and relax, to enter my inner world. I got closer to myself, which made me braver.

No giving up, no gain.

After all the arrangements, Mike and I took a road trip to the West. Traveling to other countries was challenging because of the many restrictions, but traveling within the U.S. was much easier.

This trip took us twenty-one days, and we crossed seventeen states. We started from North Carolina and went through Georgia, Alabama, Mississippi, Louisiana, Texas, New Mexico, Arizona, Nevada, California, Utah, Colorado, Kansas, Missouri, Illinois, Kentucky, and Tennessee, with 7,200 driving miles total. Mike drove five thousand miles, and I drove two thousand miles. I transferred from a new driver to a skilled driver. I could drive in any kind of conditions. I remember when we drove to Denver, our car was sandwiched between big trucks. Then it snowed, and the car slipped. I had to be patient and focused.

In Texas, we stopped at a small restaurant on the side of the road, and the staff did not wear masks. When we asked them why, they said they had never worn masks since the pandemic. We were very shocked. It seemed the different states had different rules, and people here practiced more free will. It was great to drive 80 or 85 miles per hour in Texas. I enjoyed the high speed.

During this trip, I met volunteer mates Aldeana and Pedro in LA. Aldeana was a second-generation immigrant, and her parents were from Jamaica. We lived in the same house for a while when we volunteered in Malawi. She earned her master's degree in architectural design just as the pandemic started.

She shared with us how frustrating it was to search for a job in 2020. She drove from Chicago to LA but couldn't find a full-time job in the architectural field. Instead, she worked as a part-time babysitter. The pandemic kept more children at home, making it difficult for parents to focus on their jobs, which increased the demand for babysitting.

Pedro was a second-generation immigrant as well, and his parents were from Latin America. He was on the same team as Aldeana. When Aldeana volunteered in Malawi, Pedro went to Mozambique. He had a good heart and high energy and was eager to help others. During the pandemic, he quit his full-time job and worked at a few part-time jobs. He applied for an online master's degree to improve himself. He gave us more energy.

On the way to San Francisco, I met my client, Clara, who was also a career coach. Originally from Shanghai, we first met at the Global Career Development Conference in 2016. After that, she became my client and later a trainer for my training project, where she shared insights on career development in the American job market.

She told me that when the pandemic began, she started working from home. During that time, she also began leading an online dance club, teaching Christian worship dance. She found joy and meaning in this activity. When I asked her how she viewed aging—since many Asian women experience age anxiety— she simply said,

"Age is just a number!"

So wise!

Everyone adapted to the pandemic in their own way, and for some, it opened doors to new possibilities.

At the end of our trip, we spent two nights in Denver. The city had a peaceful energy that helped me unwind and relax. We enjoyed delicious food—from fresh seafood to a cozy French restaurant—and even treated ourselves to full-body massages at a Chinese massage place.

With that good energy, I spent one morning taking the online PCC (Professional Certified Coach) written exam from ICF. I had submitted my application a few weeks earlier, and everything went smoothly. Two weeks later, I received my PCC certification.

What impressed me the most about this road trip was that in just a few hours, we encountered different weather: sunny, windy, rainy, snowy, and hail. I was so worried about driving in the heavy snow and could not see the road clearly, but in the next few minutes, everything was fine; it was a flat road, and sunlight was coming. I could not believe it. It looked like the universe played a game with us and showed me that change is inevitable and this, too, will pass.

The end of one journey is the beginning of the next!

Part Two
The Neutral Zone

Chapter 8
What Is Happiness?

Starting on April 1st, 2021—thirteen months after the pandemic began—I entered a new stage: taking a break. At forty years old, after running for so many years, I finally gave myself permission to pause.

Mike and I had savings, which allowed me to rest. I didn't know how long this break would last, but I accepted that life had brought me to this moment.

But just because I paused my business didn't mean I could slow down right away. I was like a fast train that had come to a sudden stop, but due to inertia, the train continued moving forward. I still worked very hard on my social media and individual clients. It wasn't until six months later that I could slow down a bit.

In William Bridges' book *Transitions: Making Sense of Life's Changes*, he describes the transition process in the following stages: Endings, The Neutral Zone, and A New Beginning. I came to The Neutral Zone stage, and I knew this process was suffering, but it had its own meaning: letting go of the past and nurturing the future.

But I was confused. I had two main sources of confusion. The first one was direction. What was my next direction? Did I need to do my business in the U.S. or work for an American company? I did not have the answer. What I knew was that I needed to rest and have a break, then go on the next journey.

The second confusion was what I was looking for. What made my life meaningful? What was my life's purpose? What was happiness? I was in my forties. I had had many experiences, and now I had come to this corner.

When I stopped my busy schedule, I started paying attention to myself. I found that without work, I could not stay calm—I was very emotional. Usually, I had one or two days of peaceful time. But for the next three to four days, my energy would be turbulent. I felt angry and stressed. Sometimes, I would just lie on the bed and read a book for a few days until I finished it. When I completed the book, I felt even angrier and sadder.

Without work, all the patterns of emotion came. Even if I gave myself permission to take a break, I could not enjoy it. I felt even more anxious than before.

It looked like I was pursuing happiness, as other people did. What was happiness? I had a traditional opinion: if I worked hard to achieve success in my career, then I would get happiness. This meant that success brought happiness.

I created my business, and I made reasonable money. I was surprised that in the fourth year, our total income reached seven figures, and our costs were 40 percent of income as we operated online. I had more time and money to travel, but I did not feel happy. I felt more stressed. I questioned the traditional opinion about happiness, and I was on my way to finding the answer.

. . .

I watched many Buddhist talks about life wisdom. I realized I was very greedy and had a big ego. When our team income reached seven figures, I immediately wanted eight figures. Did I really need that money? No, I just wanted to prove I was good.

I also read the novel *Siddhartha* by Hermann Hesse, originally published in 1922. It was about the spiritual journey of self-discovery of an Indian man named Siddhartha. It showed everyone had their own way of finding their path. Experiencing was a good way to attain enlightenment. I was not sure whether I understood this book, but I agreed that our own experience was more important than what we were told.

I also read another book, *The Book of Joy,* in which I found the answer to being happy. This book is a heartwarming conversation between the Dalai Lama and Archbishop Desmond Tutu, facilitated by Douglas Abrams. These two spiritual leaders discuss how to find lasting happiness despite life's struggles.

The book names eight pillars of joy: perspective, humility, humor, acceptance, forgiveness, gratitude, compassion, and generosity. From this book, I knew:

1. If you want to be happy, you need to learn how to be happy. You will not attain happiness automatically. In our lives, there are no textbooks about happiness, and we think if we have a wonderful family, money, a decent job, and social status, we will be happy. Or that if you suffer too much, you can become a Buddhist. When we approach a new job, we go to training. But when we pursue happiness, we don't learn the way to be happy.

2. You need to build a mental health immune system. Usually, we spend a lot of time exercising to build our physical immune system, but we don't know how to build our mental health immune system. When you have a strong mental immune system, even when something difficult happens in your life, you're still able to maintain a positive attitude.

3. Modern education focuses heavily on brain training, such as analysis and competition, while often neglecting heart training, like emotional awareness, human connection, and compassion. But people feel happy more easily through the heart, not the brain.

4. There are four pillars for happiness from the mind (perspective, humility, humor, acceptance), and there are four pillars connected with the heart (forgiveness, gratitude, compassion, and generosity).

I was so fond of this book that I could not stop reading it. I felt very peaceful. I also knew why I was not happy. I used too much of my brain and did not pay more attention to my heart. I could not even feel my heart in my daily life.

I was very glad to explore happiness and to look for the answer and practice, not just be told by others.

When I explored happiness, I began reflecting on both my business and personal life. When I looked back on my business, I realized I had gone down the rabbit hole. I watched YouTuber Vanessa Lau's video about her own rabbit hole, and I felt we had a similar situation. She had been a video creator for three years, but she paused her business for one year because of burnout.

When I started my business, I followed the pattern of "the more it is, the better it is." Every year, I launched a new program, believing that constant creation would make my business—and bring me more happiness and security. But instead of feeling that way, I only became more exhausted.

Leadership was my biggest challenge, and I was busy and unable to develop it, perhaps even avoided this part. At the same time, I didn't practice self-care, and I didn't know how to be good at it. I was always unsatisfied with myself, and I criticized myself a lot. I worked hard but never earned my own approval, and finally, my body protested.

Running my business felt like being on a fast train. I could not stop, and I put fuel into the train often. The problem was that I didn't know where I wanted to go. Next time I build my business again, I will start differently. Enjoying each day—not just chasing speed—will be the most important thing.

In my personal life, I felt I had only been happy in the time before I went to school. In my childhood, China was not developed. I lived in a rural area. Parents paid little attention to their children as they had a lot of work to do. My job was playing, and I played with my sister and brother, nature, and dogs. It was a great time!

Since I went to school, I knew this game: I needed to have an outstanding performance to gain my parents' and teachers' love and attention. Then, I started years of competing, and my happiness depended on my scores.

In 2000, I completed the Gaokao which was one of the most challenging experiences of my life. I was accepted to a university. The first two years felt like a brief break where I enjoyed the campus life. But in the third year, I realized it was time to prepare for my future career.

I started to run, and for twenty years, I never stopped to rest. I was running and running, exhausted. The pandemic came, and I did not want to run. I wanted to stop for a little while.

I was that girl who was running, fighting with life, and trying to stand out from the competition. The life had become a competition machine. When I reached my forties, I felt I could gain more strength and wisdom to choose—to live the life I wanted: easy, joyful.

There's a Chinese saying from Confucius:

"At forty, I had no more doubts."

At forty, I turned inward, seeking answers and truth from my inner resourcefulness.

Chapter 9
The Story of Losing a Cat

I n September 2021, eighteen months after the pandemic started, Mike went to visit his parents in the UK, leaving me at home with our two cats. I applied for a visa back in August, paying extra for expedited processing, but it hadn't been approved yet. I didn't know then that this time alone would become a lesson in separation and connection.

One night, when I returned home after swimming, I saw Hope but didn't see Freedom. Suddenly, I realized I hadn't seen Freedom all day, and I quickly checked if I had any recent dreams about Freedom (it was a habit of mine; whenever something happened, I checked if I had any dreams that might have foretold it).

I remembered a dream a few nights ago:

Freedom and I were visiting my parents, and they really liked him. On the way back home, Freedom was walking ahead with a silver chain around his neck. Suddenly, he disappeared, and I found him under the bed. A black child had grabbed him, hiding under the bed. I paid the child, and Freedom came back.

This dream stuck with me when I woke up, and I even wrote

it down in my notebook. But I didn't understand its meaning. Now that this had happened, I still felt very anxious and scared.

Without Freedom, Hope kept meowing incessantly, making me restless. After dinner, I took a flashlight and a snack box and wandered around the neighborhood, but I didn't hear any cat cries.

The next morning, I told Mike about the situation, and he immediately posted a missing cat notice on NextDoor, which is a neighborhood-based social media platform. He suggested I search the neighborhood in the morning and advised me to take Hope to walk with me and look for Freedom.

Hope had become very timid, always returning home on her own after a while. She ran to my feet, meowing, and seemed afraid that I might leave too.

I took Hope for a walk. Passing through a grove of trees, I heard a cat meow, and it sounded like Freedom's. I approached and saw a British Shorthair. Hope cautiously approached, and the British Shorthair also approached her.

Suddenly, the British Shorthair leaped and attacked Hope. Hope ran away, and the British Shorthair chased her. Before I could react, Hope had darted under a car, with the British Shorthair in hot pursuit.

I heard Hope's desperate cries. She had been bitten. Soon, she scrambled out from under the car and dashed up a tree, closely followed by the British Shorthair. As she climbed the tree, I arrived in time and shouted sternly at the British Shorthair, who jumped down and ran back under the car.

Hope sat at the top of the tree, trembling, making fearful noises that she usually made when chased by a dog.

I was shaken and afraid the British Shorthair might attack me, too. I chased it away from under the car and stood guard under the tree. It took a long time to coax Hope down.

I walked her back, and she was exhausted and panting heavily. I sat on the ground, trying to calm my racing heart.

We continued, no longer searching for Freedom; getting Hope home safely was the priority. Further ahead, we encountered an old man walking his dog. Hope was afraid of the dog. She saw a drain and immediately jumped in. I ran to the drain in shock.

The drain was about three to four meters deep, with only a few footholds on the cement wall; the rest was slippery. How could Hope get out of there? She looked up at me, terrified, and cried out.

I didn't know if I should call the property management to open the drain. I tried it myself. The rectangular cover was heavy but could be moved. I asked a few neighbors crossing by to help me open the cover.

I grabbed the handrails on the wall and descended to the bottom. Hope had run to the other end, screaming. It was pitch dark in that section of the drain, and I had no light source.

I climbed back up and gestured to a woman to lend me her phone. She understood immediately. I used the phone's light to peer into the drain, and Hope remained where she was. The drain was only large enough for one person to crawl through, and I was too scared to do it.

I went back up and moved to the nearest drain. Hope's head was poking out from underneath, and she was crying out in fear.

I asked another neighbor to help me open the cover again, injuring my hand in the process. I didn't care about the injuries; I just wanted to rescue Hope.

The area around the cover was filled with soil, and when I lifted it, the soil fell in. I climbed down, but Hope wasn't there anymore; perhaps the falling soil had scared her away.

The space was very narrow, with barely enough room to sit, let alone crouch. I called for Hope, but there was no response, just silence. I realized these drains were interconnected throughout the neighborhood, making it difficult to know where Hope had gone.

I squatted there, feeling hopeless, guilty, frustrated, scared, and heartbroken, tears streaming down my face. I asked myself:

"Why do I create such an experience? Losing one cat isn't enough? Do I have to go through losing another one?"

I cried and called out, but there was still no response. I went back home to see if there were any solutions. As I climbed out of the drain, there was no one around.

I walked home feeling dejected, intending to return later to cover the drain. When I reached the house, I suddenly saw Hope standing outside the backyard fence, weakly meowing at me.

I was overjoyed; I picked her up and couldn't help but cry. I carefully checked her — she had no injuries, just her body trembling from the overwhelming fear. I thought she was lost, trapped in the drain and unable to get out. I never expected her to climb out on her own.

I carried her back home, exhausted, and collapsed on the ground. Hope lay quietly beside me, watching me cry. After calming down, I locked Hope inside the house and went back to the drain with tools.

In the afternoon, I stayed at home with Hope. I had a short nap and was suddenly awakened by Hope climbing onto my chest and sniffing me. This was her way of testing if I was still breathing. She had done this before, just to see if we were still alive. This was how Hope showed her love for me, afraid that I might be too sad and die!

As I sat quietly that night, having a conversation with myself, I wondered why I had to go through this separation experience at the same time. Suddenly, I thought I should contact soul communicator Liqin for a session. I felt there was an issue I needed to address.

The session was quite long. I'll summarize the communication briefly.

"Your soul says that your role in this matter is multi-layered. You are both a teacher and a student. Through this incident, you're creating a learning experience for yourself. This is very positive," Liqin said.

"This event has also magnified your belief in separation and how you uphold this belief in relationships with others," Liqin continued.

"I have always felt that separation is a theme, that people and relationships will eventually separate. Because I know everything will eventually end in separation, I don't want to invest emotionally anymore. Someone once said that I seem very enthusiastic on the surface, but it's hard for me to get close emotionally," I said.

When I talked about this, all my memory was awakened: when I was in elementary school, my siblings transferred to another school, leaving me alone in the old school. Then, I made a good friend in fourth grade, and we were inseparable. I met a math teacher who appreciated me, filling some of the void left by my father's lack of love.

But in the first semester of fifth grade, we moved suddenly, and I had to transfer to a new school. I never properly dealt with this separation trauma. For many years after, I often dreamt about my elementary school teachers and classmates.

Before university, my family moved four times. After graduation, I moved countless times on my own, changed jobs, and later moved across cities and countries, switching industries and deepening my belief in separation.

"Your low spiritual energy relates to your beliefs. Because your spiritual energy is low, your heart is closed," Liqin said.

I also felt that my heart was closed, and that I was more comfortable being alone. Over my years of coaching, I had to constantly replenish my clients' energy, which lowered my energy. To protect myself, I closed my heart. When my spiritual energy was low, opening my heart made me vulnerable to hurt.

"Your weak spiritual energy is related to your excessive use of logical thinking. You're good at using your brain and focusing more on planning and goals, which weakens your spiritual energy," Liqin said.

Yes, I had always been a logical thinker, and I benefited from it as a student and in my career as well. But the logical thinking made it hard to connect with other people deeply, including myself.

Now, I was slowly transitioning to a heart-led approach, but most times, my initial reaction was still logical thinking. I needed to spend a lot of time meditating, conversing with myself, and not letting myself be led by plans and goals.

"The viewpoint of separation between people, the lack of connection, leaves people rootless, lacking strength. If you feel connected to others and everything around you, you will take root in the earth and be filled with inner strength," Liqin said.

Yes, I live in a world with many kinds of separation:

You and I are different. I'm rich; you're poor.

You and I are different. You're white; I'm black.

You and I are different. I graduated from a prestigious university, broad-minded; you graduated from elementary school, narrow-minded.

You and I are different. I'm from a developed country; you're from a developing country.

I suddenly realized the modern society's loneliness epidemic was a sense of separation. We had become unable to connect with others, with nature, with everything around us, living solely in our minds, seeing everything as separate and disjointed. Even surrounded by many people, we still felt lonely. Originally, we're all human, but we're divided into different categories, labeled differently, and driven by logical thinking.

My brain often plays out scenes like this: when I wanted to reconnect with old classmates, I thought,

"Oh, we live in different cities. Their thoughts might differ from mine. We might not have much to talk about."

When I wanted to reconnect with old colleagues, I thought,

"We're not in the same industry anymore, and we don't have common topics or interests."

My brain was constantly judging, calculating, trapped in a loop. I yearn for this state: I'm joyful, accepting, without judgment towards others, and able to communicate happily with anyone. That person may have many patterns, but as long as my heart is open, it's fine.

After completing the soul communication, I paid Liqin 1800 yuan ($280). She was happy with the payment, and I respected her value.

The next morning, when I got up, Hope started meowing again. I opened the back door, and she went out. Suddenly, I saw Freedom standing next to Hope.

Freedom was back!

I didn't know where he came from, but I went up to him and petted him, tears of joy streaming down my face. I felt his fluffy fur again.

I understood the meaning of my dream. The black child who grabbed freedom represented my separation belief. In the dream, I paid the black child, and in reality, I paid Liqin, and then the cat came back. I really directed this entire scene myself, but before directing, my dreams gave me a hint. Freedom really loved me and supported me in creating such an experience.

As I was chatting with an old friend, I told her I used to be open-hearted towards her, but because of some things that happened, my heart closed off to her. I told her all these feelings, expressing my concern for her. I felt like a channel in my heart had opened again. She was happy for me, and she said her heart had always been open to me.

Then, I sent a message to my elementary school classmate. I often dreamed about her but never told her. This time, I poured out my feelings from these years to her, expressing my concern for her. I felt like another channel in my heart had opened again. We've never been separated. We all cared about each other, although we did not meet very often.

Separation was created by my brain, and I had enveloped myself in a glass shell of separation. Now, I was opening this shell, stepping out, and breathing in the fresh air outside.

It was all thanks to Freedom. He is not just a cat to me; at times, he seems wise, watching over me. Sometimes, he plays the role of a parent, and other times, he plays the role of a child.

This whole experience felt like a play written and directed by my subconscious, with a dream dropping clues along the way. I wasn't just an audience member—I was also the scriptwriter, the director, and the actor. In losing and finding my cat, I began to see more clearly: the stories we live aren't random. They are shaped by us—by our beliefs, emotions, and the lessons our souls are ready to learn.

Chapter 10
The Methods of Releasing Emotion

When I had my time, I tried to do many things—writing in my diary, meditating, connecting with nature through gardening and camping—and especially connecting with myself. I found that the past issue annoyed me. When I thought of Tong Zhou's event, I still felt furious.

When I had this emotion, my brain tried to reason or persuade me to be positive. But I could not stop to think. I always tried to find the solution to the emotion, which did not help me release it.

This time, I tried to go deeper. I found this anger was not about her; it was anger at myself. I was angry about why I was not smart enough to avoid this thing and why I had made this mistake.

The same thing happened to my clients during coaching sessions. When they talked about their relationship, they were furious with their friends or partners, and finally, they found they blamed themselves. Why did I know this person? Why didn't I see this person clearly? Why did I become friends with this kind of person? Why did I have a relationship with this guy? It goes on and on.

When I found my patterns, I realized that the emotions I had been experiencing stemmed from my belief that I was not good enough. I was angry with myself.

One day, when I read negative news about China, I worried. I said to myself:

"You are not there; you had better start your new life. You even paused your business. Why is your heart still there?"

The more I said, the angrier at myself I became. I even wanted to slap my face to punish myself to release the anger. This thought shocked me. Deep down, I really hated myself. When I watched TV dramas or movies and saw people actually slap themselves, I was shocked by how harshly they treated themselves. Now, I even had that thought. It was common.

In the book *The Art of Happiness: A Handbook for Living*, the Dalai Lama asks the author why modern people hate themselves, as he had not had that experience. When I read this, I thought about the people who experience modern education, learn to overuse their brains for everything, and compete with others. There's a side effect of this education. It teaches us not to accept ourselves.

One day, when I read the book *Emotional Balance: The Path to Inner Peace and Harmony*, I came across the following sentence:

"After 30 years of dealing with sick people, my conclusion is the following: all inner turbulence (emotional stress) comes from self-rejection."

Yes, this happened to me. I had an experience. It hit me.

The author shares where this self-rejection comes from.

"We all have a so-called self-judge, which we normally hear as a voice in our head. This inner judge is the by-product of our upright caregiver or parent who was our boss when we were young for survival. When we grow up, this becomes inner parents."

I needed to please my parents because I had more siblings. My strategy was an excellent performance in school. This caused my parents to have high expectations of me and for me to have high expectations for myself. I think most Asians have the same issue. The Chinese clients I coached, who worked in American companies, all had this issue.

I realized the positive relationship I needed to build was the one with myself—I needed to love and accept myself. In the *Conversations with God* series, author Neale Donald Walsch says that all your relationships with others just let you see who you are. Other people are mirrors. I understood it. When I have emotions about others, it always comes down to my not accepting myself. You may dislike someone because there is a part of yourself you also dislike.

I practiced the forgiveness tool from the book *Emotional Balance: The Path to Inner Peace and Harmony* for two to three weeks, and I felt better. I experienced no more anger with myself. Here, I share how to do this:

1. Tap the liver point, which is on the right side, halfway up the arc of your ribcage while saying, "I deeply love and accept myself with my anger (or resentment, or feeling of revenge) toward (the offender)" at least three times.

2. Tap the kidney point, which is next to the breastbone, under the clavicles, while saying, "I deeply love and accept myself with my fears that something like this might happen again" at least three times.

3. Tap the heart point, which is next to the cuticle on the inside of both little fingers, while saying, "I deeply love and forgive myself for creating this incident, and I forgive (the offender) for being part of this, and I let go of this, now and forever" at least three times.

I finally understood that forgiving other people was forgiving ourselves. When you hate other people, you put yourself in jail. I was glad I had released myself from the jail. Later, when I coached American clients, I found most clients trapped in emotions they didn't know how to release. Sometimes, they did not know they had emotions. Through my active listening, I could feel that they had them.

Usually, I gave them time to connect with their bodies, as the body recognized the emotion. I let them be quiet with their emotions and their bodies. Some clients said they felt fire or black energy. They watched for a moment quietly. The fire got low, and the black energy (like messy yarn) got small. I let them keep watching. They found it disappeared, and they became more peaceful. This way, I let the clients observe the emotions and not label emotions. With no judgment, you can just let it go.

I developed two methods to release my emotions.

The first one is: connect with my body.

Usually, when I feel emotion, my stomach or belly may give me a signal (hiccups). I find a place to sit quietly and check inside myself. Then, I try to talk to my subconscious to find the reason. Most of the time, the subconscious gives me the reason— connects with my previous experience. I cry and release all my emotions.

The second one is: observe my emotions.

I sit on my mat quietly and breathe deeply. I watch the emotions in my stomach area like a mist in the valley, rising slowly and then disappearing. Usually, I practice it for ten minutes. The mist rising and disappearing, the new one rising, disappearing...

The more I practice, the more aware of my emotions I become.

The book *A New Earth: Awakening to Your Life's Purpose* suggests that emotion is the body's reaction to your thoughts. Our body is very brilliant and connects with universal intelligence. It gets all the wisdom from the universe. You don't run your body; the intelligence does.

This intelligence gives rise to the instinctive reaction of the organism to any challenge. For example, when we encounter a lion, our heart beats fast, and we may run fast, which surprises us.

Emotion can be a response to an actual situation or event, but it will be a response to an event seen through the filter of the thought. It will relate to our values, judgment, and experience. For example, someone might meet a stranger alone, signal to the body "danger" and become very nervous and stressed. Someone may not have this signal and keep very calm when talking to a stranger. They might even make a friend.

I had an Asian client who told me that when he was on the subway or at a meeting, he felt terrified of being surrounded by crowds. He had to leave, and if he couldn't, he would faint. I gave him quiet time for over five minutes, and he found the answer on his own: his brain said it was dangerous and gave the signal to his body.

This client worked in finance, and he had to make sure all the numbers were right. He trained his brain to notice even slight mistakes. Gradually, his brain was like a mongoose, and any little thing happening sent him the message:

"Danger, run!"

Through our body's reaction, we may know our thoughts, our egos, or our limiting beliefs.

From my coaching experience, Asian clients and white clients find it more difficult to connect to their emotions, while African Americans and Latinos find it easier to connect to their emotions. The former also has more difficulty connecting with their bodies.

. . .

Releasing emotion became one of the most powerful tools in my personal growth and coaching work. The more I explored and embraced my emotions, the more I could live with inner peace and self-compassion.

I learned to meet them with curiosity, listen to their messages, and gently let them go. Once I learned how to free myself, I was able to help others do the same. This journey not only brought clarity to my emotions but also illuminated the profound interconnectedness between personal growth and professional efficacy.

Chapter 11
Shanghai's Lockdown

When other places released restrictions, China was very strict with the COVID-19 policy. In March 2022, authorities locked down Shanghai, and two of our team members were there.

We had a meeting to support the three coaches (one was from our training program) in Shanghai. Their life was okay, but they were emotional and had low energy. One coach shared that under intense pressure, she almost broke down and burst into tears with her partner. She could not believe it would happen in Shanghai. The gap between reality and imagination confused her.

Every day, the rumors and the sad videos from the WeChat group made them more stressed. They were born in the 80s, and they had never experienced an event like this in their lives.

The lockdown confined my two nieces to their small apartment. They came downstairs for the COVID-19 test and could see the sky and the flowers. Many people had similar experiences. A COVID test was a life routine.

I contacted my classmates and ex-coworkers, whom I had not been in touch with for a long time. Lockdown connected us.

They were safe and had food. They could not go outside except for the test. When I talked to one of my university classmates, she told me,

"I appreciate I have a habit of storing stuff. This time, it really helps me!"

I checked in with one of my former coworkers. He told me he wasn't in Shanghai and was on a business trip in a northern city, lucky to have escaped being trapped.

When I read most people's WeChat moments, I could feel their anger, depression, and fear. Only one was different. It was a coach who practiced Buddhism. She seemed full of acceptance and calm. She also tried to show positive energy to other people.

I sent her a message:

"I thought I needed to comfort you. But from your WeChat moment, you are good."

She replied to me,

"I am also slowly learning. Recently, I seem to have returned to Shanghai during the Republic of China era in the late 1930s. I have seen hoarding in history and experienced this phenomenon."

She accepted this event from a broad perspective. When people shift their perspective and look at the same thing from a different angle, they realize that not everything is as it seems. This connects to *perspective,* one of the eight pillars of joy. When people change the angle to see the same thing, they may find calm.

Shanghai's lockdown had a huge impact on me, thousands of miles away. I had an affection for Shanghai, as I started my business there and had my wedding there. Mike and I had lived there for four years. The lockdown news shocked me. Whenever I read the news or listened to people discussing in the WeChat group, I felt so heavy.

I felt my emotions. I found that I had never let China go, even though I had not been there for three years and had paused the business. My heart was still there. When something happened, especially negative news, I would spend days researching it.

We were always educated to love our birth country. I felt like China was my mother. I thought my mother should be the perfect mom. But she was not. Then I felt angry and depressed, as though there was negative energy between me and my birth country. But I still loved her deeply.

I understood that most immigrants had the same issue: even after we were physically separated from our birth countries, we still carried emotional ties filled with negativity.

I talked to an immigrant originally from the Middle East about what he felt about his birth country. He had been in the U.S. for over forty years. His children were all born in the U.S. He sighed and said the country's situation got worse and worse. He felt very worried and disappointed, but he could not do much.

It does not mean when we grow old or stay a long time outside, we will let our birth country go automatically. We have negative emotions connected with our birth country, like disappointment, anger, and so on, especially if we come from a developing country.

I told my soul communicator, Liqin during one session that I felt hopeless about my career transition to the American market. Because I could not let China go, I could not live my present life. I thought this was the most difficult transition in my life. She said:

"Your soul wants to tell you that separation from your birth country is a very important thing in your life. You need to give yourself more time and be more patient!"

Yes, I felt this was a big separation. It was so hard, and I needed patience.

The ironic thing was that when I called my mother, she still thought I was in danger and worried about us a lot. She always complained about what happened to her with my brother. She did not have a good relationship with my brother.

This time, I was furious. I felt terrible every time after talking to her. Maybe for her, worrying about me was a kind of love. But I felt she did not know me, never understood me, and did not want to spend time getting to know me.

I was an adult, and I knew what was good for me. I could take care of myself very well. Mike has lived in the U.S. for over twenty years, and he knew more about the country than my mother. My mother just watched the news and came to us to share her worries. I felt she was showing me she did not trust me to make a good choice to move to the U.S., and now, she had to worry about me.

I asked myself why I needed to call her every month. The reason was filial piety, which was Chinese culture. If you don't do that, you are not a dutiful daughter. Then I talked to myself:

"I don't want to be dutiful like this. I want to make myself happy."

I decided not to call her again.

For the next six months, I didn't call her.

I felt better that I had built the boundary. When my sister asked me why I had not called, I said I felt bad when I called her. They understood because my mother called them to share all her negative emotions. But they lived there, and they could not reject my mother's phone calls. This was a typical relationship between mothers and daughters in many Chinese families. Daughters become the mother's emotional trash can.

Finally, I said no.

. . .

One day, suddenly, my subconscious reminded me to pick up the book *Emotional Balance: The Path to Inner Peace and Harmony*, and I reread the part about emotion.

This time, I had a good understanding: emotions were free radicals. They were not very stable, and they were stored in our bodies, especially in our chakras. When something happened, it was the trigger for the emotion. This book called it the "pain-body" or unresolved emotion.

When I lived in China, I attached many emotions to my experiences and stored them in my body. I was very easy to trigger. What I needed was to release the emotions. When I did not have these emotions, these triggers would no longer hook me. This time, I tried the powerful emotional healing formula to release my emotions.

This emotional healing practice incorporates the chakra system, which comes from ancient Indian spiritual traditions. It describes seven energy centers in the body, each linked to different physical, emotional, and spiritual aspects of our well-being. When energy flows freely through these chakras, we feel balanced and aligned. But when the flow is blocked—often by stored emotions or past trauma—it can lead to discomfort, emotional reactivity, or a sense of disconnection.

The process is as follows:

1. Affirmation: I accept myself and deeply love myself with my fear of letting go of this feeling. I accept myself even if I will never let go of this feeling completely.

Inhale and exhale deeply. Focus on Chakra 1: The Root Chakra.

2. Affirmation: I ask my angels and guides to assist me to the origin of this feeling (negative emotions). However long ago, and help me to heal this completely.

Inhale and exhale deeply. Focus on Chakra 2: The Sacral Chakra.

3. Affirmation: I allow every part and aspect of my being to assist me in healing this original incident, however long ago, and to completely accept and love the original intention.

Inhale and exhale deeply. Focus on Chakra 3: The Solar Plexus Chakra.

4. Affirmation: I forgive myself, by the love of God, for rejecting myself and others, for my incorrect beliefs, thoughts, feelings, and perceptions, and I forgive any person, incident, others, and anything involved, and let go of any reason or belief to need this any longer or at any time during any of my past experiences. I have allowed the healing to be complete for all related incidents ever since.

Inhale and exhale deeply. Focus on Chakra 4: The Heart Chakra.

5. Affirmation: I now let go and release with unconditional love and God's blessing all of the old that was part of my feeling or thinking this way, now and continuously. I choose to replace this with (positive moods). I accept this feeling of (positive moods) in every cell of my body.

Inhale and exhale deeply. Focus on Chakra 5: The Throat Chakra.

6. Affirmation: I am giving myself permission to let go of any related discomfort on a physical, emotional, mental, and spiritual level or any related attitude, behavior, or feelings with ease and grace, now and continuously.

Inhale and exhale deeply. Focus on Chakra 6: The Third Eye.

7. Affirmation: I thank God, my guides, and my angels for all their help and express to them my love and gratitude. I accept and am worthy of all of God's blessing and love.

Inhale and exhale deeply. Focus on Chakra 7: The Crown Chakra.

Tip: In Step 2, write the emotions you're currently feeling and include them in your affirmation. Then, in Step 5, choose a new mood to replace those emotions. For example, if you feel anger and disappointment toward someone, you might replace them with acceptance and peace. Use the emotion words in Step 2, and the new mood words in Step 5.

I had practiced for one month, but then I found that I was not very emotional. This was a powerful tool. The next month, I found I had other emotions (the emotions have different levels), and then I continued to practice. To my surprise, when I thought of China, I felt very peaceful for three months.

I accepted what was. China has thousands of years of history, and she has her own journey. I didn't need to worry about her.

I realized I also felt worried and guilty about my family members. I continued doing this practice. I felt more peaceful. Before, I wanted to save them, as I thought they did not know the truth and that I knew more than them. When I felt peaceful, I thought that was their journey, and I needed to respect it. No bad, no good, no judgment.

I found that I gradually stopped going to YouTube to watch negative news about China. The invisible hand that always wanted to grab me to the news disappeared. Since 2023, I haven't watched any negative news. Without these negative emotions, I felt free of my experience, and I could focus on my present life.

This lockdown changed people's relationships with Shanghai in different ways. Some experienced loss, some experienced gain, some experienced emotion, some experienced awakening, some experienced appreciation, some felt trapped, and some experienced freedom.

One of my university classmates was a professor at a university in Shanghai. He studied in the U.S. and then moved back to China before the pandemic. After the pandemic, he brought the whole family back to the U.S.

For me, it was a great gift to see my deep emotions tangled with my past. Through my efforts, I was free of the past.

Most people who are in a big life or career transition have the same issue as me. We can't let our past go because of the negative emotions we associate with it.

If you're struggling with this, try this emotional healing formula. This tool can be used anywhere, in any situation that creates emotions. Here, I summarize my application:

1. Relationships. This can be interpersonal relationships, intimate relationships, relationships with children, relationships with parents, relationships with the system, relationships with yourself, etc.

2. Trauma experienced in the past. Being laid off at work, betrayed or hurt by someone, laughed at because of failing a test, afraid to drive again because of a traffic accident, or afraid of entering a new relationship after being broken up with by a scumbag are all examples of trauma. Maybe you've experienced a failed marriage and no longer trust men or are grieving the death of a relative or loved one.

3. Meet new challenges. Learning something new, leading a new project, building a new company, making a large-scale transformation, immigrating to a new country, and having a baby and becoming parents are all examples of new challenges.

4. Emotions arising from some emergencies. This includes being robbed, attacked, having an accident, being injured, etc. When you think about these things, you no longer feel negative emotions. Instead, you feel peaceful and may wish the best for

anyone or anything that has harmed you. It means you let it go. You break the negative connection.

The negative connection I had with China was an enormous obstacle when I tried to start my new career in the U.S. Once I released it, I felt peaceful. I no longer needed to worry about it.

Many immigrants struggle to fully open themselves to their new country because their hearts are still tied to their birth country through worry, anger, and other negative emotions. It's not about trying to change your birth country to satisfy you—you will never be fully satisfied that way. What's more important is changing how you relate to your birth country: accepting it as it is.

When you accept your birth country, you also accept a part of yourself—the part that shaped your past. Only then can you truly open yourself to exploring new countries.

Chapter 12
Dog Walking

I never expected that in the years 2021 to 2023, I would learn such important life lessons from animals. I became aware of my beliefs about separation when my cat Freedom went missing, and the dogs at the animal shelter taught me something profound about love.

I started volunteering at an animal rescue center in November 2021. I found playing with my two cats very enjoyable, and I wanted to play with more cats. I registered as a volunteer at the Humane Society of Charlotte and attended training sessions.

At first, I mainly did cat socialization, which meant playing with the cats using toys and petting them to help them feel loved and prevent psychological problems.

Being a dog-walking volunteer was conditional. You needed to clean the dog kennels four times, each time for three hours. It took me almost two months to complete these four tasks. This job was really tough; it wasn't easy to earn the chance to walk the dogs!

During each kennel cleaning, there was one staff member, and the rest were all volunteers. We had to prepare food for different dogs, mixing dry food with wet food.

When I entered the kennel, standing in that narrow space, it felt really cramped. Life as a shelter dog wasn't easy. The hardest part was dealing with dog poop. Some dogs just pooped anywhere, and it was often runny. And some produced a big pile that smelt terrible. I never wanted to have a dog because I didn't want to pick up poop, but now I had to face it.

Wearing gloves and double-layered plastic bags, I could still feel the soft, warm poop, making me nauseous with its strong odor. I almost threw up several times but never actually did. After picking up enough poop, I gradually got used to it, calmly picking it up with the bag and throwing it into the trash can.

During this process, I met many volunteers, including an Indian high school student, a girl who planned to study biology in the future and showed interest in STEM. I also met two Chinese girls adopted by American families, both in college and volunteering in their spare time. They did not speak a word of Chinese, both being girls abandoned in southern China around the year 2000 because of the one-child policy. A few years later, when I coached American clients, I had several female clients who were adopted from China.

When I started walking dogs alone, I usually checked the descriptions of the dogs at the door and chose ones that were relatively small, gentle, and preferably female. I tried to avoid mouthy and jumpy dogs as much as possible, as they were hard to control.

Sometimes, the other volunteers took all the easy-to-walk dogs, so I had to choose male pit bulls. These guys were tough. They just rushed out as soon as they were out and dragged me along. I even slipped once.

Usually, we took the dogs to the yard first to let them walk around and play for a while. These dogs then behaved differently.

Some immediately started pooping and peeing, while others tore apart the toys we gave them. These shelter dogs were different from pets in regular homes.

Some were strays, some were abandoned by their owners, and some had suffered various traumas. Their experiences often explained their strange behavior. For example, there was a dog that lay on its back whenever I got close, looking terrified.

Once, while I was sitting on a chair, a dog naturally put its front paws on my legs as if we were old friends. I was surprised by how natural it felt! The way it treated me made me feel very trusting and good.

I walked a very old dog named Kevin, a German Shepherd who was around nine years old. He couldn't have any treats because of health reasons. I took him out, and he walked quietly with me like an old friend. This reminded me of 2014 when I volunteered in Michigan. Mette, a Danish staff member, had a German Shepherd named Mila, who provided me with a lot of emotional support. In the later stages of volunteering, there were many draining disputes, so I took Mila for a walk, spoke to her in Chinese, and poured out my troubles to her. She just listened quietly, and that silence felt like comfort.

Walking with Kevin made me feel the same way I felt with Mila: companionable and non-judgmental. This is also why people like dogs; they don't criticize or judge you; they just accompany you.

During the second walk with Kevin, an accident happened. He got very little food that day. When he saw food on the ground, he struggled desperately to break free from the leash to eat it. His elderly body exerted tremendous strength, and I couldn't hold him back.

When we got to the grass outside, he seemed a bit distracted. The leash got wrapped around his neck, so I let it go to get it from the other side. Unexpectedly, he caught on to this minor mistake. He immediately ran back. I was stunned; it was the first time this had happened. I chased after him, but he was already far ahead. A passerby saw this and shouted.

Kevin ran to the gate of the shelter, which was closed, and he couldn't get in. At that moment, a staff member came over and grabbed him just in time. It turned out he wanted to run back to the shelter to eat! If he had run elsewhere, it would have been a big problem.

Later, when the shelter moved, he came out at the grand opening with "adopt me" written on him. He was adopted shortly afterward. While I was happy for him to have found his forever home, I couldn't help but feel a bit lost, knowing I wouldn't be able to walk him again.

In April 2022, two big dogs arrived—fluffy, tall, and gentle. I liked them a lot. Later, I found out they were Akita dogs. They were siblings returned by their adopter, mainly because the owner couldn't handle them. I didn't dare walk them alone.

Another volunteer, Kim, walked with me, one dog each. When I led the sister out of the dog kennel, I felt a special sense of richness. I finally had the chance to walk such big dogs! It was amazing! It was so lucky! I almost burst into laughter, feeling so happy.

They had good temperaments and were chubby, fluffy, and had a kind of silly and cute feeling. When I crouched down to hug them, they stood quietly. Touching their soft fur, I felt a special aura, and tears streamed down my face. I felt like something was about to burst out of my heart, but I didn't know what it was. I had this feeling for several days.

On April 10th, during a coaching session, I talked

to Hellen about this feeling. As I spoke, I suddenly realized that feeling was a strong sense of love trying to flow out, a feeling that wanted to burst out of my heart but encountered obstacles.

In my upbringing in Chinese culture, I never learned how to express or accept love. My father never expressed love with words to his children, nor did he hug us. The only way he expressed love was through specific actions, like cooking delicious food or giving treatments when we were sick, as he was a doctor. My mother's expression of love was slightly better, but we never got hugs from her.

With Mike, we often hugged and expressed ourselves verbally, but mostly through actions. It seemed like I had never experienced that passionate expression of love, and my emotions had been suppressed.

From my experience, the people who can express their feelings passionately are Latin Americans and Africans; they express affection passionately—through kissing, dancing, and rich body language. In contrast, many Asians tend to be more reserved when it comes to expressing their feelings through body language—whether it's kissing, hugging, or dancing. As many Asians age, their bodies become stiffer, and their faces appear less expressive.

These two Akita dogs, with big hearts and bodies and soft, warm fur, had pure energy. When I hugged them, their tremendous energy broke through my internal barriers. My emotions burst out, my heart opened, and tears flowed.

That wasn't the only time a dog helped me open my heart. Hellen had a Labradoodle, Thor, whose parents were therapy dogs. She previously told me Thor could provide healing. Thor was a very tall dog, sleeping at the moment. When Hellen walked over and hugged him, he just followed along, completely trusting, with no struggle. His shape changed with Hellen's way of hugging, like a clay doll.

I watched on the video call, laughing and crying at the same time. Hellen and her dog showed me that love was about trust, not struggling or judging, just going with the flow.

This special coaching session made my heart excited for a long time.

I shared this coaching experience on my WeChat moments, and a client specifically messaged me, saying she also struggled to express love. Her husband enjoyed expressing love, but she felt uncomfortable and didn't know how to respond. I suggested she be bolder and learn how to express her own version of love.

Gradually, I no longer feared those mouthy and jumpy dogs. When they jumped up and licked me, it was all about expressing emotions, expressing their love. Sometimes, I would choose big dogs to walk, and that feeling was very strong. When they jumped up at me, instead of avoiding them like before, I hugged them head-on, and they didn't dodge the kisses either.

This feeling was superb. I was able to bravely respond to their way of expressing love and send out my love in return. I caught their love and gave them mine, a brave and passionate love transmitted between humans and animals.

In January, when I shared this experience during the coaches' personal growth sharing, Yali said her son sometimes hugged and kissed her, and she would feel very uncomfortable, even afraid of his snot getting on her.

Children and animals are the same: without judgment. They express their love innocently. However, when children express their feelings so passionately, we may not respond as bravely and passionately as adults.

I often took the dogs to the dog park and let them run free without leashes. I threw a ball, and they sprinted over to grab it with their mouths and run back to me. I felt they were my dogs, my friends. I didn't feel like a volunteer at all, and I did not feel like they were dogs from an animal shelter.

The book *Emotional Balance: The Path to Inner Peace and Harmony* talks about how one important aspect of being human is learning to love—learning to love unconditionally, without judgment. Animals showed me what unconditional love was. All the relationships in our lives—with parents, children, siblings, friends, bosses, subordinates, and clients—are opportunities for us to learn love.

Thanks to the dogs I had walked for over a year, on the surface, I volunteered to support animals, but on a deeper level, they supported my life growth, supporting me in learning to love.

According to *The Book of Joy*, one pillar of joy is generosity. Volunteering is the practice of generosity and time given. Yes, this made me happy and opened my heart to others. I was on a new journey to practice a new way to be happy.

Chapter 13
Going to the UK

In May 2022, after twenty-six months of the pandemic, I went outside of the U.S. for the first time to travel to the UK. Even though we had been vaccinated, I was so scared. I used a mask most of the time, even on the airplane.

I had not traveled internationally for over two and a half years. We transferred at JFK Airport in New York, where there were a few people. I had received a phone message about a case of COVID on the plane, which made us a little nervous.

We arrived the day after Anne and John had come back from a cruise in Portugal, which was their first overseas trip after the pandemic. It was good to meet them again. The pandemic kept people away.

John's Alzheimer's disease, which was diagnosed in 2016, had grown worse, and he couldn't express himself very well. Mike's brother and sister-in-law both got COVID-19 earlier in the pandemic, and they were very seriously ill.

Anne coughed a lot and thought she had caught a cold during the trip, but then she tested for COVID-19, and her result was positive.

She had caught COVID!

That's why she had been coughing. One morning, she mistakenly took Mike's coffee and said that the tea tasted weird. We thought COVID was far from us, yet now it was so close. Still, we were calm as we got the vaccination. Anne contacted her family doctor, and she just needed to wear a mask if she went outside. We lived together normally, and we treated her as if she were a normal person.

I thought,

"If I have to get COVID-19, please let me get it after the Global Career Development Conference in June."

I got it after the conference.

We had a good time accompanying Anne and John. Mike had become a freelancer and a math tutor, and we both had flexible time. The pandemic changed people's careers, as many people worked at home, which was a totally different experience. Many people made a slight career transition—from full-time work to part-time work or contractor or freelancer work.

Anne had a dog called Sammy, who was nine years old but looked like a puppy. His previous owner was a boy with autism. Sammy experienced a lot of trauma, and his best hobby was eating.

When we walked him to the market, he went to the corner, and then stopped. He wanted to come back, and he liked to walk with John—the old man and the old male dog had a strong connection. We had to give him a treat to lure him. It worked sometimes. Other times, he was like a stubborn old man—stiffening his neck, protesting with his feet, and refusing to go. His feet were like nails driven into the ground. We had to bring him back.

We had our own time to travel around, and I liked this part. British parents give more freedom to children, and they respect their children's space.

We went to the Chelsea Flower Show, which had reopened for the first time after the pandemic. The Chelsea Flower Show was incredibly crowded. People had been trapped for a long time, and they were eager to return to normal life.

It was the Queen's Jubilee, which was a big holiday. When we crossed the street, we saw huge flower decorations on the doors of the stores. All the different variations of roses attracted me. They were gorgeous. After this trip, I even changed my vegetable garden to a rose garden.

We rented a car to start our trip to the north of the UK. When we were ready to go, we found Sammy sitting in our back seat. His other favorite thing was sitting in the car to go someplace. If Anne and John brought him out, he might get food in a restaurant or have some other exciting experience. Anne had to pull him back hard.

Poor Sammy!

Our destination was Edinburgh. On the first day, we just randomly stopped at a small town called Stamford. The town was unique and quiet (most English towns are unique), and the buildings were old. Stamford was ranked among the top 10 places to live in the UK. We were so lucky to be there. We went to a very old bookstore, and I found some books printed several hundred years ago.

Later, we went to the county show. It was amazing. It was an animal get-together, with hundreds of lambs, sheep, goats, cows, horses, dogs, and pigs (I didn't see a cat) all coming to compete. This was my first time attending a county show. There was good food and some entertainment and different shows: a sheep haircutting competition, a horseshoeing contest, monster trucks demolishing abandoned cars, horse shows, bird shows, and dog herding.

I saw sheep I had never seen before, and I even saw twenty piglets inside a small cage. Their mothers needed to join the competition, so they came here for the show.

Everybody was happy.

I enjoyed walking in the Peak District. You just opened the door of the farm and then walked. Sheep were near you, and they ate and nursed. Life in the countryside was so peaceful.

The weather changed fast. One minute it was sunny, and the next minute, it was raining. We had to stop next to a small wall under the trees. A few brown lambs hid there for shelter. I squatted by the wall, and then I found a white lamb walking directly to me. I was so surprised. When it came to my front, it turned back and ran.

I understood I was like her mother. I wore white clothes and a white hat. When I squatted, my side was like a white sheep. When the lamb came close, it found it had made a mistake. I enjoyed the feeling of being like their mother, even though I couldn't give them milk.

We traveled to Manchester to visit Mike's university and the Manchester City Football Club. I was not a football fan, but Mike was. Maybe most English people have their own team.

Mike's team was Ipswich, and he spent a lot of time watching games every week. I had never seen him play the sport. If I were a fan of some game, I could play it. I understood that football blood went deep into the English DNA.

In small corners, I saw some special things for fans. Some fans died, and their family members brought their pictures here so they could still see their team. I was very touched. Stones were marked with words in remembrance of fans who had passed. Even death could not separate them from their club.

In Mike's case, football was the connection between him, his father, and his family. When he was young, his father brought him to watch the game. I think football has a connection to many families.

In Liverpool, we visited The Beatles Story Museum. It was so great to know more about this famous band. We went to the Cavern Club, where The Beatles performed earlier in their career. Anyone could give the name of a Beatles song to the musicians who worked there, and they would perform the song. I liked the song "Let It Be." At first, I did not understand it very well, but now I know the wisdom of "Let It Be."

Yes, it was acceptance!

Mike and I drove to the Lake District and stayed at a small farm. There were only two to three households, and it was called a hamlet. This was a family operation. They had four to five dogs and were all open and friendly. They had a lot of lambs in the cage. There was a small pony alone on the land. The owner's daughter told me his mother died, and he was alone. He loved to be touched and had a very fashionable hairstyle—long, fluffy fur that covered his head. With his stylish mane, he looked quite handsome.

The place was old, and the road was very narrow, as it was used for wagons. When we drove in the middle and encountered another car, we had to drive back and yield the left side of the road. Mike was more polite; he always drove back when he saw the other car.

One night, we stayed at a hotel in a small village. There was not enough space for parking. We had to park a little farther away. After we checked in, the manager showed us one parking space. Then I stood there, and Mike went to drive the car.

I stood in a hatched area, marked with a yellow line and guarded by two traffic cones. The parking space was right next to me. When I watched my phone, a compact car drove into the parking space. I was shocked and trembling in disbelief at what happened. I rushed to the driver, a young woman. I told her this was our parking space. The girl said it was her parking space, which the manager had given her.

I was so angry with the girl, the manager, and myself. Why did I not stand in that parking space but next to the parking space?

I went to the manager, but she was not there. I also found another staff member and explained it to him. He followed me to the parking place, and he told me:

"The place you're standing on—the yellow line—is your parking spot. We put the traffic cones there to save it for you."

Everything got solved. It was my mistake.

Mike came and parked there. After that, my body was still trembling, and my heart was racing, like I had gone into a battle. I thought deeply about why I was so reactive. I had experienced many situations like this before. Resources were limited, and I was sent to occupy space. When I failed, the people who sent me would scold me. I felt so scared with limited resources and guilty for not having done very well. I felt furious at the people who took the resources. Whenever I saw other people take our place, I felt I had to fight. My brain thought the situation was dangerous. Then my body reacted: my heart beat fast, my voice became intense, and trembled.

I saw that I had a hidden fear of having limited resources. I also felt anger and guilt. I didn't see the world as abundant. This connected with my life situation when I lived in China. There are many people in China. Resources are limited, and we have to fight for them. When I was young and went on the bus with my family,

99

we had to fight for seats. Now people are more polite, especially young people, as they grow up with more resources supplied by their families.

When I saw my pattern, the emotion was gone. The next time I experienced a similar situation, I knew I had more resources, and I did not need to fight. The trip created more opportunities to check my patterns and to see my hidden emotions.

We arrived in Edinburgh, an ancient and beautiful city. The street was very wide, and the cobblestones gave the city an ancient feel. We just had time to visit Edinburgh Castle. Then we came back for a new experience, a canal boat trip.

Anne rented a canal boat with three beds. It was an enjoyable journey. We cooked and slept there. Usually, either Mike or Anne drove the boat. Even John could drive it for a few miles, as his hands still remembered the motions. I tried to drive it, and it was very difficult. I turned quickly and too often, and sometimes, the boat touched the bank.

We encountered different boats. There were many beautiful flowers on the roof. It was a unique experience to live on the boat, with more freedom. Then we met many animals, including cows, in the grassland next to the river. They were shocked to see us. Wild ducks liked to swim around the boat as I fed them.

A wild swan brought her babies to welcome us. Of course, we gave them good food. Sometimes, we stopped to get off the boat and find a pleasant restaurant or a pub. The English countryside was so beautiful and also a little shy. You need to find her beauty with patience and slow movements and feel it with your heart.

The fun part was going through the lock on the canal. Usually, Mike and I got off the boat to open the lock, and the boat could go inside this three-to five-meter narrow channel. After that, we closed the gate behind the boat and opened the paddle on the front gate. The water came in until the water level was even with the upper level. Then we closed the front paddle and opened the front gate, and the boat moved out. It was a brilliant idea to let the boat travel to different water levels.

When John was sitting in front of the boat, he usually slipped and could not stand. I helped him sit back. Most of the time, I picked up bunches of wildflowers to put in a bottle and then put the bottle in the boat's front.

Everything was beautiful!

When we came back to Woodbridge, the neighbor had a party for Jubilee Day. Every family cooked food and brought it to the garden. Most of the people were old, and I thought I was the youngest. Many people came to this town for retirement life. Sammy was very happy as he could have good food. I always threw the food on the ground to feed him secretly.

One couple were also American immigrants. They went to work in the U.S. thirty years ago as it was easy to find a job there. Every year, they spent a few months in the UK to visit their family. I could feel that even though they had lived in the U.S. for many years, they still thought they were British.

I could feel this from Mike. He usually listened to BBC news and watched British TV dramas that were produced from the 1970s to the 1990s. Mike's native language is English, and he comes from Western culture and a developed country. He did not suffer too much when he moved to the U.S., but most of the time, he was like a guest there.

As a non-English speaker from a developing country and an Eastern culture, I suffered a lot. Suffering has its meaning, and every experience has its value. That pain became one reason this book was born.

It has also taught me resilience and the ability to adapt to new environments, shaping the person I am today. Each challenge I faced became a stepping stone for growth and transformation, proving that even the toughest journeys can lead to profound revelations.

Chapter 14
Global Career Development Conference

In career transition, industry association resources play an important role. First, they give you opportunities to connect with other professionals. Second, they give you more company—you are not alone; you belong to a professional circle.

After I had come back from the UK, I went to Anaheim, California, for my second Global Career Development Conference by NCDA (National Career Development Association). My first time was in 2016. When I immigrated to the U.S., I planned to attend the conference. Then the pandemic hit, and all the conferences went virtual. After two years, NCDA started the first half of the in-person conference. They held the other half as a virtual session.

There, I met many coaches from the U.S. in private practice. (Many Chinese coaches could not come to the U.S., as China had not lifted its control over the pandemic in July 2022.) I attended several sessions about resilience and burnout during the pandemic. Being resilient is very important in our career field and our lives. If we treat our life as a long marathon, how can we go the distance?

During the break, I sat in the hallway for a rest. I noted an older gentleman sitting next to me. He introduced himself as Dick. It was interesting to learn that he was a professional trainer and had just finished teaching a four-hour Professional Development Institutes (PDI) training program.

When he told me he was in his eighties, I could not believe he was still working. American people work until old age. I really respect their work ethic. My father-in-law was a similar age to him, but he suffered from Alzheimer's. Working makes people healthier and helps them connect with others.

When I told him I graduated as a math major, he mentioned that Asian people were hardworking, patient, and good at math. He told me he had read a book called *Outliers: The Story of Success*, which shared this opinion. For a long time, Asian people have cultivated rice, and rice needs a lot of work and cooperation. It requires patience, detail, and hard work.

The same is true for math, which requires more patience. When I studied at university, I spent the whole night solving one math question. While coaching in the U.S., I noticed that my Asian clients excelled in mathematics and science. As Asians, we inherit the patience of the generations.

Dick said that many laundromats were run by Asian American owners, like Korean Americans. The laundry business requires more detail and makes small money. The laundromats I had gone to were owned by Chinese Americans and Korean Americans.

I went to the vendors to look for FCD training (Facilitating Career Development) because I needed to apply for my CMCS (Certified Master of Career Services) certification. In the U.S., gaining professional certification is very important. You don't have to go to university for another degree; just the right certification will give you more credibility. When you try to make a career transition as an adult, affordable training and certification can help to open the door.

I talked to a staff member named Keri, a beautiful woman with long hair. We were so happy to chat. She shared that she had retired, had just started her business, and volunteered at the NCDA Conference. We talked about family. Her daughter worked in my city. It was a small world.

After that, I went to a round table hosted by two female coaches and shared about how to start a coaching business. I saw Keri sitting there again. Those two women were business partners, which gave me the idea that I could have a business partner. I suggested to Keri that we could collaborate in the future, as we felt very open and close to each other. This was a seed.

On the last day, I met Aldeana again. She drove a secondhand car and played loud music. She was full of energy, like a butterfly on a beautiful blooming flower. We had dinner, and she told me about her new job as an architect's assistant. No more babysitting! She loved her job, and, most importantly, it paid very well. She treated me to this delightful meal. I saw how a job and financial independence could change a woman's confidence.

When I finished the conference, I took a flight back. This time was different. I did not go to the restroom even though I had drunk a lot of water. I collapsed when I got back, the headache and exhaustion too much to bear. We had a testing kit for COVID-19, and Mike helped me use it.

It was positive!

I could not believe it. I had COVID.

I went to a free public test stop for another test. It was positive, too. My wish became a reality: *if I get it, please let me get it after the conference.*

I did not have a cough, and my taste for food was normal. I didn't have a high fever and was not feeling hot inside my body. For the first few days, I just had a runny nose, and the tissues were piled next to me.

I recovered from COVID in a few days, but within a few months, I started feeling extremely sleepy in the mornings after getting up. Sometimes while driving somewhere, I had to stop every hour because I could barely keep my eyes open.

I want to reflect on what I gained from the conference.

At one session, I met the speaker Sharon, who was the current president of NCDA. She was from South Carolina and had a business in Charlotte. We connected.

She started a mentoring program for new coaches, and I joined it. My mentor was Jane, who had practiced career coaching for many years. I got one year of free mentoring from her. She gave me more emotional support and confidence and let me connect with American women very well. To thank Sharon, I invited her for a meal when she came to Charlotte.

Second, Keri and I communicated further about applying as co-speakers for the next NCDA conference. We discussed the topics. Because she was busy, we ended up with an incredible result: we applied to be speakers separately, and both of us had two proposals approved—one presentation and one round table. I had thought that I would be a speaker in a few years. Because I interacted with Keri, we became speakers quickly and well.

Before the conference, I got an email from the NCCDA (North Carolina Career Development Association). There would be a network meeting for the coaches from North Carolina. I was not a member. I met Jamie, who was a board member of the NCCDA. Five of us had good food, and later, I joined NCCDA, and Jamie and I met a few times. Then, I became a speaker at the NCCDA conference in March 2023.

Also, I joined the FCD training. This was three months of online training. My instructor was Linda, who lived in Colorado. At first, there were three women registered, but then two couldn't take part, and I was the only one. I got one-on-one training.

Linda was in her seventies, and every day, she had Zoom meetings on many subjects related to career development. She was very responsible and worked hard. I respected her spirit. I had never seen Chinese women in their seventies still working professionally. They would retire in their fifties.

As I had practiced career coaching for a long time, this training was not very difficult for me.

The lesson about career transition theory impressed me as I was in transition. What attracted me the most was Nancy Schlossberg, one of the few female pioneers of career planning theory (most theorists in career planning are men). She is also one of the few theorists who focus on the field of transition. Her 4S theory of transition is well known. She was born in 1929 and is still active in the workplace, which makes her unique.

Let me explain this theory.

The four S's are Situation, Self, Support, and Strategies. When you are facing a transition, you must first evaluate your current situation, such as how long this transition will take and why you should change. Then, sort out your own inner resources, such as whether you have experience in dealing with transition and whether you have enough skills to deal with this kind of pressure. Then, look for external resource support, such as family, friends, counselors, financial support, etc. Finally, make your own specific action plan and start implementing it.

For the Self part, Nancy mentions that an individual's inner strength and experience are critical elements in coping with transitions. It means that people with inner strength and more experience handling change are more likely to navigate transitions successfully than those who lack such strength or experience.

For example, in my previous cases, individuals who had been with the same company for over a decade since graduation were often fearful of changing careers, even when they were unhappy in their current roles. When seeking a transition, they had a higher chance of returning to their old job. Those who had experienced various transitions in their life and careers were more positive and adaptable to new environments during times of change.

In this regard, some questions can help clients to sort out:

1. What does the client's overall life look like?

For example, some people just love to mess around, and some people are relatively stable for many years.

2. Do clients view things more positively or pessimistically?

Similarly, a glass of water is half full. Some people see it as half full of it, and some people see it as half empty.

3. Does the client believe that life is controlled by external forces, determined by the hand of fate, or is it controlled by oneself?

4. Does the client have adequate skills to deal with anxiety? Can they make decisions?

5. Has the client experienced effective coping with change in his/her life? How adaptable and resilient are the clients?

I applied it to myself.

Earlier in my career, I had experienced a lot of transition, from a math major to studying HRM (human resource management) online, then moving from trainer to recruiter to headhunter, becoming a talent assessment consultant, becoming a career consultant, and finally, doing career coaching. My journey took me from Beijing to the U.S., Malawi (Africa) to Shanghai, and the U.S. again. I have undergone many life and career transitions, and every time, I made them happen. This helped me to see that I could make this transition. Success cultivates more success.

After completing the course, I wrote an article titled "Four Effective Ways of Building on Clients' Inner Strengths to Accelerate Career Transition" which Career Convergence (an NCDA magazine) published in April of 2023.

After this training, I got a CMCS certification, which qualified me for seven years of full-time career coaching.

This conference marked a new chapter in my professional life. It wasn't just about learning new tools or earning certifications. It was about rediscovering my career path in a new country.

By connecting with American coaches and building a new social network, I gradually shifted my professional identity from a Chinese coach to an American coach, especially on a psychological level.

Chapter 15
Volunteering at Refugee Support Services

A fter I came back from the NCDA conference, I took one step: volunteering at RSS (Refugee Support Services) in Charlotte. I really wanted to connect with different people.

As an immigrant, I understood the challenges of learning to live in a new country. A refugee's challenges were much greater. I registered to volunteer with RSS to support refugees, and I received a quick reply. There were several programs for refugees, and I chose the KTG (Knit Together Group), where the women gathered on Thursday mornings to knit, crochet, and learn.

I decided I would like to be part of this particular women's group.

The KTG program started in 2012. They accept donations from the community, especially yarn. They organized female refugees to crochet different products that were then sold at different places, festivals, craft shows, or other big events. The refugee women are paid for their finished products, and the profits made are put back into the supply costs of the program. Female refugees can earn a small amount of money from this project, but it is their money, so it is empowering to them to have even this small earning opportunity.

On September 1st, the first day I went there, I met Annie, who was the Program Coordinator. She was like a sister. Marci, a volunteer, was like a mother who took care of everything. Marci was Annie's firm support, and she had been volunteering and working for RSS for fifteen years, but in other program areas.

I met and got to know the other volunteers. Carolyn was a stay-at-home mother, and she was very fashionable. She was so confident and different from my previous Chinese stay-at-home mother clients. I asked her,

"Are you worried about being a stay-at-home mother?"

Many Chinese stay-at-home mothers worry about whether they can find a job when returning to the workplace, their financial independence, and whether their husbands will continue to love them. Becoming a stay-at-home mother has become a high-risk choice in China.

Carolyn said no. She had work experience, and she connected with society through her volunteer work. She told me that Western culture encourages women to be more independent during their growing-up years.

Beth was a geophysicist who had worked in Alaska. I could sense that she had the strength of independence and a deep connection to nature. I was drawn to her. Val retired from her psychology work, and her life involved volunteering and traveling to different places. Audrey was a university-level dance teacher. She is the founder and artistic director of a dance company.

Most volunteers were born Americans; Vida and I were the only immigrants. Vida immigrated from Iran a long time ago, and she worked as a psychologist (we had two psychologists in our group). She could crochet very well. Sometimes, she brought blankets and slippers she had already made and taught us how to crochet them.

The refugees were from different countries: Burma, Bhutan, Afghanistan, Iraq, and Eritrea. In my mind, Bhutan has been regarded as one of the happiest countries, and I could not believe refugees were fleeing from there.

I learned about Bhutan from Chinese celebrities Carina Lau and Tony Leung's wedding in 2008. They had a big wedding ceremony there, which introduced many Chinese people to this small country.

Annie said many people were shocked, but she explained that Bhutan was a Buddhist country, and if you were a Hindu, you were persecuted, harassed, and banished from the country. The refugees from Bhutan came to the U.S. for this reason—but only after living in shoddy refugee camps erected in neighboring Nepal for sometimes over thirty years.

On the first day I saw one refugee's crochet bag, I fell in love with it and purchased it immediately. Annie was very happy, and she said most volunteers had a similar experience on their first day.

I did not know how to crochet; I had learned just a little knitting from my childhood. I learned to crochet from my new friends, and I fell in love with it.

As I came almost every Thursday, I got to know this group of refugees more and more. Most did not speak English well, and they did not have high education levels, but they were friendly and had very calm energy. Sometimes, one member from Eritrea brought her daughter. She was a toddler, and she was very quiet and played by herself. Sometimes, another refuge brought her grandchildren to play with her. This refugee was the same age as me, and she had grandchildren!

Annie said they were married very early, likely as teenagers, and became mothers very young as well. When I volunteered in Malawi, I met a woman who was younger than me and had a married daughter. She was married when she was fifteen years old, and her daughter got married when she was sixteen years old.

My volunteer job at KTG was to take pictures and make videos for the program. During the Charlotte International Art Festival, the ladies crocheted decorations for some trees in uptown Charlotte. Annie called this a "yarn bomb," and it was an amazing piece of art. This group of women had clever hands. They came to the U.S. and suffered a lot during their journeys. I heard stories from some refugees who had stayed a long time in refugee camps, and they definitely experienced trauma. But they still showed their pursuit of beauty in life.

I connected with Rana, who was in her seventies and was very good at crocheting. She was from the Middle East. We could not understand each other, but we could use body language.

Sometimes, she crocheted beautiful items, and I bought them from her. Rana was an excellent businesswoman in her country. She knew how to promote the items she made to me, but I did not know how to reject her "sales pitch" if I did not want it. With the help of Annie, who knew the ladies better, I learned I needed to bargain with her. I practiced it, and I felt better. I was happy to support Rana, but if I didn't want to buy something, I just had to learn to say "No."

Every Thursday morning, I felt very happy. I drove for over forty minutes each way to RSS. When this group of people were together, the room was full of energy. We talked, and we laughed. I liked to look at everyone's products and take pictures of good ones. Since I was an immigrant and good at communication, I could talk to everybody easily.

One day, some guests visited us, and every volunteer shared why they wanted to come here to assist with RSS. We all mentioned the great emotional support we felt here. Yes, I felt more energy here. I devoted my energy and got energy from them in return.

I could feel that this group of women had a different energy from the professional groups of women I had been around. The RSS ladies were more humble and very natural; they lacked ego. Their energy was like a quiet river, flowing slowly, not resisting, just accepting and adapting. When I was there, I felt accepted and not pushed.

I have always liked to observe the women I am around. Usually, Marci and Annie were very busy and rushed, taking care of paperwork and administrative functions. Vida and Beth always looked for something to do. If there was nothing specific to do, they felt frustrated. They were born in the 1950s, 60s, and 70s. Carolyn, Audrey, and I enjoyed doing something specific, but we also enjoyed not doing much of anything, just talking and observing. The three of us were born in the 1980s.

Women who were born in different eras have different values. The women who were born in the 1950s, 60s, and 70s want to do something, and they place a lot of value on working hard. I have American female clients who were born in this time period, and they show the same behavior. They always try to keep busy and stay busy. Their brains push them to always do more. For those of us who were born in the 1980s, we enjoy "doing" but also enjoy "being."

My work at KTG was a special way to offer support through presence and energy. I also observed that refugees from Burma usually sat together, and women from Eritrea liked to be next to each other and converse with each other in their own languages.

. . .

One day during Easter week, Marci finally had time to sit. She sat with Val to twist yarn and chatted about when they were young and how they prepared for Easter. Other people chatted or crocheted. The children played. At that moment, I had a feeling that took me back to my childhood when a group of women enjoyed their casual time and their children played around them. Marci and Val were knowledgeable women in this female community, and they exuded a very stable and warm energy, much like older female family members of mine. I was like a little girl among those female members, listening to them chat and feeling so safe and relaxed.

I was very emotional. I felt very warm, and that I belonged there. Although we were from different backgrounds, we all shared a special connection. They were my family members, and they were my peers.

Sometimes, we had a party, and everyone brought food to share. One day, three women from Eritrea cooked nice food and coffee, and it was a beautiful way to share their culture. Some ladies came to these parties wearing their nice traditional dresses; it made me want to have one.

During one party, I sat next to Titi, who was from Eritrea. She told me she had four daughters and that her husband was an Uber driver. There were six people in her household, and only one person was the breadwinner. I asked her:

"Are you anxious about your finances?"

I knew that if this was the situation in a Chinese family, they would be very anxious.

"No, God blesses us!" she replied with a laugh.

I was very surprised. She showed her wisdom and positivity.

When I was in Malawi, I found people were happier even if they were not rich. But in my culture, the more we have, the more anxious we are. We lack strong feelings of security.

When I shared this conversation with Mike and asked him the same question, he said he did worry.

And I was worried, too. As immigrants, we were new here, and we did not make the same as before. The cost of living was much higher in the U.S. So, Africa was magic in my mind. I had my experience volunteering in Malawi and learning from the women from Eritrea, and though I didn't know if this was true for all Africans, the people I met had the spirit and ability to enjoy their lives despite having fewer resources.

While volunteering at KTG, I developed a special friendship with Beth. We both liked nature, especially plants. She and I each have many plants at home. She said that now that she was in her fifties, she no longer cared about how other people saw her; she cared more about her feelings. Mike's sister-in-law told me the same thing. Age brings women more strength and wisdom.

One day, when Beth and I met in a park, she shared with me that she thought one refugee didn't like her. I asked her why. She said this refugee never talked to her. I explained:

"I think she wanted to connect with you, but her English was not good, and she was very shy. You are a white woman, and she is from a developing country without a strong culture. Being with you, she may feel she needs to look up to you."

As immigrants from developing and non-English-speaking countries, we have a psychological disadvantage being part of a minority group in the U.S. We tend to feel that we are so new to this place and believe that people are very strong here. We don't know the language and culture very well, and we feel like guests who are not sure how to behave. The safe way is to keep away from the majority.

Sometimes when I meet tough, strong, white women, I feel a little nervous. If they don't understand what I say and show their lack of patience, I sometimes feel bad about myself and blame myself for the poor interaction. My young Asian clients have told me they have felt very nervous about talking to their older white male coworkers or bosses. This psychological disadvantage occurs because of society, history, and economy.

I once shared this with my mentor, Jane, and she told me she had the same feeling about Mexican immigrants.

Through my explanation, I hoped Beth knew more about immigrants' feelings.

I was inspired by seeing all the crochet products my new refugee friends made, and I started my own projects, which included crocheting a dress. I followed a YouTube video and spent six months making it. This was the first item of clothing that I made. When I posted it on my social media, my university roommate commented:

"I could not believe it. I remember you were the clumsiest one in college."

I could not believe it either. When I let myself relax, my creativity and newly learned skills came out on their own.

Through this volunteer experience at the Refugee Support Services Knit Together Group, I connected deeply with American women from different countries, economic statuses, and education levels. This experience helped me coach American women later, as I felt more comfortable and closer to them. Before this volunteering experience, I felt very distant from most American women.

From being with this group of women refugees and seeing their beautiful handicrafts, I saw their beautiful hearts and their growing hopes to make a better life for their offspring.

True connections come through the heart and the sharing of beauty and acceptance without judgment.

Chapter 16
English Study

The biggest challenge that most immigrants face is language. When many professionals immigrate to the U.S., they change their careers from white-collar to blue-collar because of their inability to speak English. I read news stories about a Chinese professor who took up a cleaning job, a financial analyst who became a DoorDash delivery driver, and a tech executive who switched to truck driving. Women may stop working and stay home to take care of their children.

Behind the language issue is the culture issue. When you are not very familiar with a new culture, or you don't like the new culture, you might feel uncomfortable speaking English.

I had the same problem. Even though I had volunteered for one and a half years in an English-speaking environment and I had been with Mike for eight years, working as an English coach was still a big challenge.

The job requires a greater understanding of cultures and good English. I felt that if I had a normal job, like an engineer or accountant, it would have been easier to handle. But coaching focuses on conversation. I had a big fear that my English was not good. I had a fixed mindset about my English.

Later, when I coached many clients from different countries who had been in the U.S. for more than ten years, they still thought their English was not good, even though they studied in the U.S. I realized most people who were not born in the U.S. had this common issue.

My struggles with English are as follows:

First, I couldn't believe I could speak good English. I learned English when I was in middle school. After a decade of studying, I could not talk to a foreigner.

Our study focused on grammar and reciting words to pass the English exams. This was how most Chinese students learned English. My brother-in-law was my English teacher when I studied at a middle school. When he met Mike, he spoke no English.

This experience of learning English made me feel hopeless. I bought many materials and purchased some courses, yet I couldn't keep studying. This time, however, I needed to start my career in the U.S., and I had to solve this problem. I had a lot of motivation, but it could not help me remove the limiting belief that had tortured me for decades.

Second, I didn't know an efficient way to improve my English. I tried studying new words, reading books, watching TV, and listening to the radio, but my spoken English didn't improve.

Third, people could not understand me when I spoke English to them. Usually, they asked me to speak again, or they showed very confused faces, even after I repeated what I said. They still didn't get it, which hurt me. I lost my confidence in talking to other people and tried to avoid it.

Now I know the reasons:

First, I spoke English quickly (I speak Chinese quickly too).

Most of the time, I was not sure how to pronounce some words, so I tried to say them as quickly as possible.

Second, I never emphasized any words, and I did not have intonation. I said sentences with flat and short sounds, and it looked like I was very unhappy.

Third, I had word pronunciation confusion. When I learned English, we used British textbooks and British pronunciation, which was very different from American pronunciation in many words like olive, sock, and black cat. One day, when I talked to an American coach about *mantras*, she looked very confused. I realized I pronounced it in a British way. When I changed my pronunciation to American, she immediately understood me.

Fourth, I couldn't understand the American people very well. They said long sentences, and I tried to pay more attention to every word, but they didn't emphasize every single word. I was lost.

One day, I read an article about a good way to learn English: imitation. Other people share the same idea. Children use imitation to learn language when they are young. Even though they don't know how to write and read, they can talk and understand other people.

I watched several ten-minute TED talks. I listened carefully, imitated every sentence, recorded my voice, and listened again. It helped.

In 2022, I bought a course for American accent training called *The Clear English Academy* from an American teacher named Keenyn Rhodes. I desired to explore the American accent deeply. I have watched her videos on YouTube for quite a long time, and I like her style; she is very elegant and very calm. Later, when I had her lessons, I found out she was a fan of Marie Forleo, and I was too.

This course introduces the American accent systematically, including vowels and consonants, intonation, placement, and more practice, which made me understand American accents deeply. I know why some people can speak good American English and some people can't.

I am very impressed with breath and placement. Before this lesson, I didn't know why I liked the American accent. This lesson helped me understand the reason.

The American accent resonates more in the mouth and throat area. A lot of other languages or even other varieties of English resonate higher in the head, behind the nose, and in the cheeks.

Also, all the pronunciation makes you open your mouth wide. I remember my friend's daughter, who immigrated to the U.S. when she was young. When she spoke the Chinese character "大" (dà, which means big), she opened her mouth very wide, which impressed me.

In British English, people produce the sound from the upper part of the head or the nasal area. You can't hear clearly, and sometimes, it shows a little arrogance. When I discussed this with my client working in London, she said,

"When British people speak, if they can avoid opening their mouths, they choose not to open their mouths."

In that case, they produce sounds through their noses instead. When I asked Mike to pronounce some new words, I rarely got them as his mouth did not open wide, and the sound was not very clear.

When I got my haircut at a Great Clips hair salon, I shared this knowledge with a hairdresser who was an African American woman. She was very surprised. She had never known this, even though she was an English speaker. She was proud of being American when she heard what I mentioned.

Of course, many Americans like the British accent. Sometimes, when Mike and I went outside and met some American people, they asked where Mike came from and then said,

"I like your accent."

I think they were saying a lot: I like the UK; I like the status of being British; I like the royal family and the queen; I want to have a European lifestyle; or maybe I like the way you speak.

It is very easy to speak American English, and for listeners, it is very joyful to listen to American accents. Hollywood movies and American TV dramas are very popular around the world. I think language is one of the important parts. When you listen to the accents, they feel very natural and smooth.

Keenyn used the same methodology to teach English: listen, imitate, and record. All the practice material helped me to do this. I even imitated her in every lesson. I think many teachers don't know the right way to help people with their spoken English. Many ESL teachers still teach grammar and reading, but it does not help with spoken English.

This journey helped me discover myself more deeply. I found that I had negative emotions while studying English. When I started this course, I wanted to follow the schedule perfectly. But after four weeks, I couldn't make it. Then, I followed my pace, and I found I fell behind a lot. I was very stressed. Also, it was very difficult to spend thirty minutes studying English every day. When I sat down to practice English, the emotions that came from my previous English study experience revisited me. I felt angry, frustrated, anxious, and hopeless.

I avoided those emotions, and I didn't want to continue studying. I was stuck for quite a long time. Finally, I practiced the

Emotional Healing Formula tool again for more than one month to solve this problem. I released most emotions, and I felt it was peaceful to study English. Gradually, I trusted that I could speak good English.

I spent five months finishing all the lessons and practice. In February of 2023, I started it over for the second time. When I practiced the "R" sound and "Dark L" sound, my tongue did not work very well. I found some tongue-exercise practice videos on YouTube. I did tongue exercises before each English practice, and over time it became more flexible. The tongue needs muscle training.

Language was my biggest challenge in starting my career in the U.S., especially spoken English and listening skills. I conquered this challenge. I felt I had finally climbed the highest mountain, and then I came to the flat land. I could walk, run, and play. It was so great!

With this course, I delivered my first professional presentation at the North Carolina Career Development Conference in March and presented another two topics at the Global Career Development Conference in Chicago in June. In my personal life, I felt freer living in the U.S. I made more friends with people from different backgrounds.

I think there are four important factors in learning English. They are:

1. Strong motivation
2. The belief that you can make it
3. An efficient method
4. Consistent study

From my experience, I think the most important factor is the belief that you can make it. Consistent study is also important. The limiting beliefs about learning English come from different sources:

1. A terrible experience studying English.

2. Thinking one is too old to learn.

3. A fixed mindset about learning English: "My English is not good now, and it will not be better in the future."

4. Perfectionism. Trying to master English in a short time.

I heard many first-generation immigrants had difficulties communicating with their children. One of my friends told me she knew a Chinese-American family. The father had a PhD, and he had to use Google Translate to talk to his children, who were born in the U.S. and could not speak Chinese.

I had a male client who worked as a software engineer in Silicon Valley. He shared with me that one of his distractions was that he could not communicate with his son very well because of his poor English. He worked hard to make more money to support his son's future. This was the only way he showed his love to his son. But for affection, he felt very distant from his son. He had moved to the U.S. in his thirties and had given up on studying English after he got his job.

Learning English is a long journey. Native English speakers have learned and used it for decades. It is very difficult for immigrants to master the language in a few years. However, you can try to improve your English at work and in your daily life. When you become more confident with your use of English in your job and daily life, you can start in other areas: reading, writing, or your hobbies.

Learning English requires a powerful belief system: I can do it. This belief is the foundation that keeps us going when the process feels slow, frustrating, or overwhelming. From a scientific perspective, belief activates the brain's reward system, boosts motivation through dopamine, and supports neuroplasticity—the brain's ability to rewire itself and learn new skills at any age. With this belief and perseverance, we don't just learn English—we open doors to confidence, success, and new possibilities.

Chapter 17
Red Rash

After the NCDA conference, my connection with American coaches grew stronger. I joined the NCCDA and had an in-person meeting with local coaches. I felt a little far from China. This separation brought up emotions that slowly built up in my body without me realizing it until my body finally showed me.

On September 27th, 2022, after thirty months of the pandemic, COVID-19 restrictions were lifted in my state. We no longer had to wear masks in public spaces. I went to the Humane Society of Charlotte for the cat socialization volunteer program, and I had a good time with the cats.

After I came back, I developed a red rash on my hands. I knew it was not an allergy as I had done this for a long time, and I also had my cats. But the next day, it became worse. A rash covered my face and my body. It was so itchy, and I wanted to scratch. I thought I might have to go to the hospital if I didn't recover the next morning.

At night, I sat on the mat to connect with my subconscious. I used a tool called Communication with the Subconscious from

NLP (Neuro-Linguistic Programming). I thanked my subconscious for always supporting me, and I wanted to talk about it again. It took a while.

For a moment, I suddenly realized that it related to the process of separation from China. I was so scared to separate from China. China had my back in my career and in my relationships with others. Now, China was going slowly. I could not stop this process, and I did not mean to do it. This was a big loss, an inevitable loss. I cried because of fear, love, and sadness.

At that moment, I imagined that my role models, Oprah Winfrey and Bill Gates, came to support my back. They told me:

"Don't worry, you are always supported!"

After all the tears were gone, I felt calmer and more peaceful. I put on the gloves to prevent myself from scratching, drank hot water, and went to sleep. The next day, all the rash was gone, and I had recovered. Once again, I built more connections with my body. She just wanted to show me my hidden emotions, and the red rash was the language.

I was amused about why it happened. In early fall, I felt more homesick for China. Fall is the harvest season, and we have many kinds of fruits, such as dates and persimmons, which are very rare in the U.S., as well as fresh peanuts and sweet potatoes. From those harvests, I felt deeply connected with nature.

China is an agricultural country, and throughout its long history, people have built a deep connection with nature. Usually, we have different types of food in different seasons that are in harmony with nature's rhythm. It was in the fall that my connection to nature felt most alive in my memory.

In the U.S., I usually could not feel a difference shopping at the grocery stores the entire year. I could not feel the change of the seasons or a deep connection with nature. Eating dates, persimmons and peanuts, water chestnuts, and Chinese chestnuts was my vivid memory of the fall. Now, those were further from me. This kind of loss made me sad.

A few days later, I was feeling an emptiness in my back, as if something was missing.

During a session with my coach, Hellen, I shared this feeling with her. After listening carefully, she invited me to focus my attention on my back. It felt like every capillary in the skin of my back was open, begging for love, for touch, for comfort. But I could not reach it. Hellen invited me to imagine that she was sitting behind me. I could lean against her, and she would gently place her hand on my back through the virtual screen. I felt terrified and tired, but imagining her hug and touch from behind made me feel safer. She had a strong feminine side, like a mother.

After this session, Hellen gave me homework: to gently touch my back. I asked Mike for gentle touches on my back for a few days, and I felt so relaxed and supported. Mike was one of my biggest supporters. Finally, my back felt calmer. Each capillary was like a contented child, receiving comfort and caresses from its mother. It went from anxiety to peace. I felt very peaceful with my back.

I realized that China had always been behind me, supporting me, and now it was gone. My back had felt empty. But when I found new support, a sense of calm returned.

In the following coaching session with Hellen, I had a new vision:

A fence blocked the river, holding back the strong current. I knew the water was powerful and that the fence wouldn't last forever, but I didn't expect it to happen so fast. One moment, the fence was standing strong, and the next, the water broke through, rushing forward. I felt nervous as I watched everything change so quickly. The flood came fast, and soon my old house was underwater.

With my house destroyed, I had to figure out what to do next. So, I took pieces of wood from the wreckage and built a small boat. It wasn't easy, but it gave me something new to move forward with. I set off in this boat, floating down the river, leaving behind what was lost. After a while, the river opened into the sea. As I sailed farther, I came across a larger ship. I knew it was time to let go of my small boat and climb aboard this bigger, stronger ship.

With my new ship, I sailed into the ocean, ready for the next part of my journey. The sea was vast and full of possibilities, and even though I had lost my old home, I felt hopeful for what lay ahead. This journey was about rebuilding and embracing the future.

"What does that river mean?" Hellen asked me.

"My life flow!" I answered.

"It was so strong and could not be stopped by the fence. The fence was my past. My old house represented my career in China. I could not continue, and I had to build a new boat to start a new journey."

"What does the sea represent?" Hellen asked me again.

"The sea? I think it's the American workplace, big platform, and gigantic space."

It looked like I was forced to do that. When I followed my life flow and let my past go, I would go on a new journey.

Part Three
A New Beginning

Chapter 18
Starting My American Career

O n December 19th, 2022, Mike and I traveled to Cuba. This was the first time we had traveled outside the U.S. except to the UK.

Cuba was the eighteenth country I had visited. We spent ten days in Cuba and traveled to different cities by bus. I arranged the trip as I was a backpacker, and I did this very often.

In Cuba, people suffered from the pandemic. There were few people traveling there, and prices were rising. Beautiful, brightly colored, old American cars filled all the streets of Havana.

We saw street cats everywhere. When we had food on the street, three kittens came for it. They were very thin. I gave them rice, and they did not like it. They just wanted my fish.

Usually, we saw people waiting outside the grocery store with some notebooks in their hands. One friend told me they had to buy food and other stuff with tickets—food tickets, clothing tickets, and so on. This happened in China in the 1960s, and I had always heard stories from my parents about shopping with these tickets. I had never seen those tickets. It surprised me that it still happens in Cuba nowadays.

We went to the grocery store, and there were a few things there, but we could not find drinking water or toothpaste.

When we stayed at a casa in Trinidad, the owners were a young couple. They had only one son. I was curious about whether the mother wanted to have a second child, and she said no. The cost of raising a child was very high, especially for the child's clothes. She needed to spend $20 to $30 on each piece of clothing. It was very high for them as we spent $30 for one night's stay.

I got an impression of the City Prosecutor in Havana. When we walked at night on the street without lights, Mike's phone was robbed, and the police officers took us to the police station.

We waited a long time for the City Prosecutor. Finally, she showed up around 11 p.m. She shared her happy moments with her daughters and even acted out how Cuban-Americans greet old friends returning from Cuba. She was so funny, and I thought she could have been an actress. She complained about her salary of just $40 ($5,000 in local money). I did not know how they could make a living. But they did, and they were not so stressed. The City Prosecutor laughed all night, and when we finished the process (we knew we could not get the phone back), she and another clerk drove us to the hotel. She had high energy even in the middle of the night. I still remember her funny performance and loud laugh.

In the street, there was loud music, and I even saw people dancing in the bar. Even a pedal tricycle owner, wearing very shabby and simple clothes, had a huge stereo in his tricycle and listened to Latin music. On one side, they were poor, and most people wanted to come to the U.S.; on the other side, they were happy and enjoyed the moment. This felt like a kind of life wisdom.

We went on a cigar tour in the Vinales area, and the guide

showed us how to make a cigar. He mentioned that many cigar farmers needed to apply for construction nails to build roofs for storing their cigars. The metal supply was very limited, and many farmers did not get it because of the pandemic. Then, they could not plant their cigar plants. I did not know that small construction nails had affected the cigar's production.

The guide was very energetic, and his English was very good. He even spoke a little French as a French family was on our tour. I asked him how he had learned English. He just went to elementary school. He said he used his ears to learn English—he listened to his clients and imitated them. I had heard people talk about learning English by ear. He was an example.

My trip to Cuba helped me understand China better due to their similar political systems. But we were not as happy as the Cuban people. We did not dance or put on loud music very often. In Cuba, they did not have an abundance of material things, but they did not feel so stressed.

Another impression of Cuba was the green toilets. When we traveled to a natural cave and went to the beach, there were no public toilets. The local people told us we had to find a green toilet. We walked to a place hidden by trees and bushes, and in a rush, we finished our business. Sometimes, we had to be careful not to step in human feces.

This experience reminded me of my childhood before going to elementary school. As a child, we did not like to go to the toilet in the hot summer, as many flies flew around in the rural area. My brother and I usually went to a cotton field for our green toilet. The feeling was so free.

When we climbed up to a famous cave with a professional guide, the trail was full of trees and rocks, and it looked like no one was coming. I was surprised that they did not do any work to make the way to the entrance better. But after this trip, I really enjoyed the climbing experience. Everything was very natural, and I even doubted whether it was good to develop everything in a modern way. Primitive attractions gave us sizeable space to connect with nature.

When I came back from this trip, I was planning to start my American career. I had a conversation with my mentor, Jane, and shared with her I needed to cooperate with an American company to get to know more American clients. After that, I would start my business. My first step was to find part-time or contract work. She agreed with my plan.

In January of 2023, my Chinese team and I reopened our Basic Training Program, but I would not be a part of it. Xiaoyun Li, our salesperson, was in charge of this operation, and she gave me 20 percent of the profit. From China's side, they released lockdown at the end of 2022, and the people I knew mostly had symptoms of COVID-19. Most of my team members and family members, including my young nephew, whom I had never met in person, all got infected.

Their symptoms were more severe, including strong headaches and body pain. Some people posted their symptoms on WeChat Moments. After nearly three years of precautions, they finally got COVID-19, and they actually felt a sense of relief.

I got a cold, and it was not COVID-19, though sometimes I could not breathe because of my runny nose. It took me three weeks to recover. Later, I found out that the people I cared about had gotten COVID-19, and I subconsciously took on their pain. Getting sick myself became a way of showing love and solidarity. It was my body's way of saying, "I'm with you."

When I called my mother, she said she stayed home most of the time because other people got a cold. She refused to use the word "COVID-19." She said that the famous doctor on the TV news told us it was a cold. But by the next year, my mother was very comfortable saying,

"Your brother-in-law got a COVID-19 variant."

Also, I felt afraid of starting my American career.I knew I needed to update my resume and prepare for the interview. But I just didn't have the motivation. Every morning, I struggled to get out of bed. One voice inside me said,

"You must get up."

Another replied,

"No, I don't want to get up."

When I got up, my whole body was painful, and my whole back was especially sore. I realized I had emotions that needed to be recognized. I had not worked for another company for nearly ten years. In 2013, I quit my full-time job and joined a volunteer program. In 2015, when I came back from the volunteer program, I worked full time for a few months, and then I started my own business.

In the past, I experienced trauma while working for the company. I was stressed, anxious, and scared. Working overtime, being gregarious, office politics, various meetings, making my boss happy—I didn't want this experience again. I told Mike about my fear, and he told me that American companies followed the rules and that the employees had their rights. They didn't need me to work overtime.

I again practiced the Emotional Healing Formula tool. I used it for a month, and then I released my emotions. I solved this problem.

I knew many people got hurt from their previous jobs, and they stayed home for quite a long time because the negative emotions held them back.

Later, I met two clients who had a similar issue. One was a

Chinese immigrant. She worked as a software engineer in China, and her boss always manipulated her using PUA (Pickup Artist) techniques: she worked too slowly; she could not catch up with the team; she was not good enough. PUA techniques refer to using tricks to control someone, such as making them feel unworthy, confused, or dependent to make them easier to manipulate. Because of the criticism, she did not want to go back to work when she moved to the U.S. When she thought of the job, that critical manager came to her mind. To avoid this experience, she avoided work.

Another client was an African American who was new to her career. She connected with her boss very well. But finally, the boss fired her after a few years. She got hurt, did not trust other people, and did not want to find a job. She needed to rest. We carried trauma from past jobs, and our brains were trying to protect us from more trauma. Once bitten, twice shy. When we release negative emotions from the previous experience, then we can move on.

At every step during my career transition, I could see how my previous life affected me and how to use my resources to find the solution. Sometimes, I felt it was a rebirth. I observed my limiting beliefs and stuck and hidden emotions. During this transition journey, they came out in the sunlight, and finally, they evaporated.

The past had no power over me! I updated my resume and jumped into a new year.

Chapter 19
Imposter Syndrome Presentation

In March of 2023, I went to the NCCDA Career Development Conference. They accepted my proposal and selected me as a presenter. My presentation was called "Empowering Women to Overcome Their Imposter Syndrome." This was my first English professional presentation about career development in the U.S. The NCDA conference also accepted this topic. I needed to present twice this year.

I used my own method to prepare for the presentation: I wrote out my speech, read it aloud, and tried to recite it. I practiced by recording myself. Then, I listened to my recording. It really worked.

When I first listened to my recording, I felt very weird. Then I practiced it again. I became more aware of my pronunciation and tone, how to say the sentences, and how to emphasize my words so that the audience could get to know me better.

I even stood in front of the mirror to practice. Sometimes, I gave this speech to my cat, Freedom. He listened curiously at first, then fell asleep. I remember one speaker named Les Brown said he practiced his speech to his chickens. An animal will not say your speech is bad.

But I had one concern. If someone asked me questions and I couldn't understand them, how would I deal with it?

I shared my concern with my mentor, Jane. She told me she could not understand her cousin very well when she visited them in North Carolina because of her accent and fast speaking. When I speak Chinese, I speak quickly. Even Chinese people cannot follow me. Some English speakers have a similar problem where other native speakers cannot understand them.

However, non-English speakers might think they are not understood because their English isn't good enough. Jane suggested that I ask them to repeat their questions, say them a different way, or speak slowly. I took the advice.

That day, I was the only Asian presenter. I arrived early to find my presentation room, and the president-elect, Belinda, warmly guided me to the right place. She was incredibly helpful, even teaching me a useful trick—how to find my LinkedIn QR code. Her kindness put me at ease. I feel so lucky to always encounter kind and supportive women along my journey.

When I started my presentation, I felt a little nervous. I thought many speakers had this issue. After I told the audience I was nervous, I felt better. When I gave my speech, the words I had practiced came out smoothly and in order. I spoke slowly and clearly. It was a great feeling. Sometimes, I added some jokes and changed my posture to interact with my audience. They laughed a lot.

I shared six solutions for overcoming imposter syndrome during my speech, which were methods from my practice. They included role models, creating a new self-image, connecting with bodies and physical space, the emotional balance practice, the mantra practice, and the thank yourself practice.

When I talked about role models, I shared how my role models led me. My two important female role models before I immigrated to the U.S. were Sanmao and Ayn Rand.

Sanmao was a writer from Taiwan. She traveled around the world and lived in Africa. She wrote many influential books. I read most of her books when I studied in middle school and high school. One was called *Stories of the Sahara*. From this book, I associated Africa with the desert.

In 2012, after traveling to Turkey, which was my fifth country with one Japanese backpacker who had traveled all over the world, I felt I needed to do something. If I didn't do this, I could not settle down.

One of my career consultant peers just learned to coach, and she needed clients for practice. I was delighted that she offered me free coaching. During one coaching session, I saw a woman with a headscarf. I could not see her face, but I saw a desert behind her. The Aha Moment came to me:

"This is Africa! I need to go to Africa!"

This coaching session changed my life, and I quit my job after working for nine years in Beijing. I joined an eighteen-month "Fighting with the Poor" volunteer program in 2013. I spent six months in Malawi, next to South Africa, supporting two elementary schools in a rural area.

Sanmao's lifestyle affected me a lot. In the past twenty years, I have traveled to twenty countries, lived in Beijing, Shanghai, and Africa, and now I am in the U.S. I created my adventurous life.

Sanmao had an international marriage, and her husband was from Spain. I have an international marriage, and my husband, Mike, is British. I even used Sanmao's English name, Echo, for many years. I changed it to Esther in 2018 when I watched a documentary about how Sanmao died by suicide. I thought I needed my new life, and I wanted to be a powerful woman.

Ayn Rand was a writer and philosopher. She had a strong character, and she was rational, powerful, and creative. Ayn Rand inspired me to move to the U.S. I was thirty years old when I read her novel *Atlas Shrugged,* about a world where the most intelligent and creative people begin to disappear, revealing what happens when they stop contributing to a society that fails to value them.

The book appealed to me, so I read it every day. It inspired me with its determination and strength to build a new system when the old one no longer worked. The female character Dagny stands out for her bravery, determination, and rational spirit in her pursuit of the truth.

I searched for Ayn Rand's background and found out that she was Russian American. She came to the U.S. when she was twenty years old. I had never seen a strong woman like her in Asia. I thought the U.S. might be a suitable environment to cultivate strong women. Then I came here.

Also, I tried to be a powerful woman following Ayn. If I don't like something, I will create something I like. When I finished my volunteering program, I went to Shanghai in 2015. As an employee, I didn't like all types of meetings and office politics. Then, I created my own business in 2016 and became my own boss.

I also admired other female writers, including Hong Ying and Geling Yan—both well-known Chinese authors—and Simone de Beauvoir, the French philosopher and feminist.

When I started my business, I gained organic clients through writing articles and posting on my social media, and I had already published a book.

Female role models are very important for women. If they don't have them, they will regard their mothers or early female caregivers as their role models. Your role models can lead you further and give your spirit support in your life and career. Your role models can also serve as material to help you create a new self-image and transform your old identity from a psychological perspective.

Your role model can even lead you during a career transition. After arriving in the U.S., I continued looking for role models who reflected my evolving identity. Maleficent is very important right now. She is not a real person but a Disney character. She is powerful with big wings. She has pure love, and she is aggressive. She can be evil and doesn't always need to be a good woman. Now, I am forty-five, I no longer feel the need to always be the "good woman." Sometimes, I can show my "bad side." When I do, I feel much freer and stronger.

During one coaching session, I saw my childhood. I was a little girl, lying on the field ridge, surrounded by wheat fields, listening to insects and birds. Then I slowly changed, and I became Maleficent. I flew into the sky with my big wings.

A little Chinese girl became Maleficent!

This powerful image reflected how my inner identity was changing—from a quiet Chinese girl to a strong Western woman.

Another inspiring figure was Iris Apfel, 103 years old. Iris was a businesswoman, interior designer, and fashion icon. She had pure energy and played with her work, and she was wise and creative. I am trying to play with my work and have fun. Also, I am going to continue to work even if I am 80, 90, or even 100 years old if I live that long.

When it came to question time, one audience member spoke a little fast and used a long sentence. I understood a little. I asked her to repeat her question, and she reorganized her sentence. Then, I was quick to get her point. When we asked other people to repeat their questions, we let them know they needed to find a

143

good way to articulate themselves. Clarifying the questions can help the person asking become clearer about what they want to know.

When the presentation was over, one career coach came to me and said she thought Sanmao lived in West Africa. I put a picture of Sanmao wearing an African necklace on my PowerPoint. This coach volunteered for AmeriCorps in West Africa, and the local people wore similar necklaces. I told her that Sanmao lived in the Sahara Desert, which lies in West Africa. That moment reminded me how everything is connected.

My presentation was a good start and a success. When I saw Belinda again, she said with excitement,

"Esther, many people came to your presentation!"

Her words filled me with joy!

From my first professional English public speaking experience, I fell in love with speaking. I even thought I could try stand-up in the future. Later, I met many clients from different backgrounds who feared public speaking. Some were Asian women, some were white men, and some were European immigrants. From my experience, I have a summary of how to improve your public speaking:

1. Practice. Write your speech and recite it if possible. Then, practice over ten times and make a recording. Listen to your recording and then improve. You also can ask English-speaking people to listen to your speech and give feedback.

2. Final form practice. You should wear the official clothes you will wear to the conference and then practice. Imagine the audience is there.

3. Come to the place of your presentation to feel connected with it. Try to practice how to move in that room and how to use your posture. Build some connection with the room.

4. Before you start your presentation, sit on the chair and take a deep breath. When you start, you can share with the audience that you feel nervous. Tell yourself, "I accept the nervousness."

Because of this speech, I found my English presentation was better than my Chinese presentation. I never prepared my Chinese presentation. I just wrote my PowerPoint and then presented it, which made my speech not flow very smoothly.

I went to another English speaker's presentation. I felt she had not prepared it ahead of time. She said one sentence and then tried to say the next sentence. Sometimes, she had to change the words.

This presentation taught me that being a great speaker isn't about having perfect English—it's about preparation and practice. With dedication and intention, even non-native speakers can deliver powerful speeches that connect with their audience. The confidence I gained from this experience not only strengthened my public speaking—it also gave me the courage to pursue my next professional direction.

Not long after, I turned my attention to the next step in my journey: job searching in the American job market.

Chapter 20
Job Interviews

W hen I began exploring contract or part-time job opportunities in May, I wasn't yet ready to work. I needed to go to Chicago for the NCDA conference in June and then to the UK in July. I would be ready to work when I came back from the UK in August. But I didn't want to wait until August to apply for a job. I wanted to see what happened.

My coach Hellen and ICF Charlotte President Toni both said they could recommend me to the coaching platform BetterUp, where they both worked as contractors. I told them to let me try first. I wanted to explore new opportunities and have new experiences. On the other side, I preferred to first gain experience working in a female-owned company, as I was also a female entrepreneur and wanted to learn more from other women entrepreneurs.

I used job websites and LinkedIn to search for jobs. I submitted eight resumes, some through job sites and others via LinkedIn, and received two interview invitations, both from LinkedIn.

Thanks to my FCD training, I knew how to look for a job in

the U.S. LinkedIn is widely used for job applications in the U.S. When LinkedIn came to China, I registered for an account, and I always use it. When LinkedIn quit the Chinese market, I switched my LinkedIn account to the U.S. version. Now, I have 1.8k followers.

The first position was of a career coach who could help engineers to look for jobs. Many engineers had been laid off in 2023. In 2004, I started my career as a technical recruiter at an outsourcing company that was connected with this job.

I had my first phone interview. The recruiter's accent was a bit difficult for me to understand. But I still got most of the questions and gave my answers. There was just one question I did not get, even though I asked her to repeat it. I recorded the interview to help me improve. I listened to the recording several times and realized that the question she asked was,

"Would you mind working with the technical interview process?"

I had misunderstood it as referring to working with the technical interviewer, who was a hiring manager.

After the interview, I tried to find out which country the recruiter was from. At first, I thought she was from Latin America, as her pronunciation was like that of my teammate from the volunteering program in Colombia. I asked Mike to listen, and he thought it was from Asia, maybe from India. I also asked one of my American friends to identify the accent. She thought it was the Philippines. Finally, I found on LinkedIn that she was from Latin America.

My judgment was right. She had an accent, but she was so confident. I learned from her that to be an immigrant, confidence matters, and accent is not a big issue.

. . .

I did not get a second interview. It was fine for me as I was not very interested in this job. I got another interview from a company called Impact Group. They posted a part-time relocation coach position.

During my mentoring session, I talked to my mentor, Jane. She had worked for this company in 2008 during the economic crisis. Many people were laid off, so she worked in employee placement. A woman founded the company, and now her daughter is the CEO. This attracted me. Jane also mentioned that one board member of NCDA worked for the company. In the professional world, this was a small circle.

My two interviews went smoothly. The hiring manager for the last interview was surprised I had gone to Africa. She was from Texas and worked in Texas for her entire career. My international background and my relocation experience made me more competitive in this position. The recruiter told me they would reply to me after one week. If I didn't get a reply, I could contact them.

I felt both excited and anxious. I wanted the experience but wasn't mentally ready. I hoped I could get an offer for part-time work. But on the other side, I did not want it. I could not focus on the job, presentation, and travel at the same time.

One week later, I didn't get a reply, so I contacted the recruiter. She told me they found a full-time relocation coach for this role, but they decided not to move forward with the part-time role. She even suggested other companies in the same industry. I felt a bit disappointed, but also relieved. I thanked them for their decision to let me focus on what I needed to do. Then, I stopped job-seeking. I planned to do it in August.

When I look back, I thank all the rejections. Those rejections let me know what I didn't want subconsciously. Your reaction to what happens to you lets you see what's on the inside. Trying is important, even if you are unsure or end up returning to your original path. This process lets you strengthen what you want and what you don't want.

This also happened when I tried to apply for a master's degree in 2021. I thought a master's degree was useful for pursuing work in the U.S. I chose MSW (Master of Social Work) as my major. For career counseling, there was only school counseling, which did not fit my area. I focused on adults. I thought the experience of studying would help me learn English and build confidence.

I spent a few months doing all the applications. Then, I focused on my paperwork, spending three days at home, writing and editing. I became so stressed that even my cats seemed to sense my tension and they lost their appetite. I felt deeply that I did not want this degree, even though I thought I wanted it. I pushed myself so hard.

The school rejected me, and I was happy. I did not need this degree. If I wanted to pursue a degree, it would be better to find some area I liked. I gave up the idea of building confidence through degree study. Working and self-development lessons have helped me build my confidence. I have practiced them consistently.

I have noticed that many of my Chinese clients in the U.S. have a similar idea: they always try to go to school for another degree when they face a career transition or when building confidence. Some even study for a second master's degree. It costs money, time, and energy.

As an immigrant, if you have a career in your birth country and you like it, you can very well use professional organizations' training and get accreditation in the U.S., and then practice. This is more useful than going back to school to study. Most academic studies cannot give you more practical experience and confidence. Jumping into the practice helps you more.

The American workplace is more open, and the employer doesn't just identify you with your previous work experiences. I met many Americans who were working in totally different roles in their careers. It is a little easier for them to change careers than it is in China.

All the rejection made me understand myself deeply.

Here is my advice for immigrants who are new to American workplaces and looking for jobs.

First, just try. Don't worry too much about whether you get the offer. If you see a position that interests you, apply. The experience of learning how the American workplace functions is often more valuable than the outcome itself.

In the U.S., many companies use LinkedIn to recruit candidates, so it's important to build a strong LinkedIn profile. If you're unsure how to start, look at the profiles of people in roles similar to the ones you're aiming for—especially those that inspire you. Learn from their profiles and use that knowledge to create your own.

Build a network in your field. Networking is useful in any place, including the U.S. Reach out to your alumni or professional peers you worked with before, and join professional associations in your field to build a new network. One of my university classmates found a job shortly after immigrating to the U.S. through her alumni network. For me, building new connections with peer coaches through NCDA and ICF helped me learn more about the coaching industry, coaching companies, and how to cooperate with the coaching platform at the beginning of my coaching business.

One of the most important steps is to practice interviewing, especially if you've never had a job interview in English. If possible, find a native speaker to practice with—it can make a big difference.

When you get rejected, don't take it personally. It doesn't mean you're not good—it just means the job wasn't the right fit. The right opportunity will come at the right time. Be persistent and patient.

After this try, I brought all my energy back to prepare for my next big career event.

Chapter 21
Chicago Trip

I was very excited about attending the 2023 NCDA Global Career Development Conference in Chicago. This conference meant a lot to me. Two of my Chinese peers would join it. Xiaoyun was my team member, and Lin Zeng was our trainee. She was my travel mate in 2010 when we traveled together to Cambodia.

I had not seen them for three and a half years. Due to the pandemic, this was their first time traveling outside China. With China's strict policy during the pandemic, we could not go back to China, and they could not go outside freely. The first time I attended the NCDA conference was in Chicago in 2016. Now, I had come back as a speaker after seven years.

I had a coaching session with Hellen before I went to Chicago. She told me she was looking for flight tickets to go back to China. All the tickets were very expensive. I felt a surge of emotion inside.

Since January 2023, China has lifted its COVID restrictions and reopened its borders. International travel gradually resumed, though it might still take time to fully return to pre-pandemic levels. I had not decided when I would visit China.

During this coaching session, I cried a lot. I appreciated all the Chinese clients who had supported me in the past decades. I had wonderful memories with my friends and classmates during my different times, like school time and work time. I felt even more love for them and more reluctant to leave. But I was going to help people from different backgrounds to experience a new life, so I needed to jump into my flow. Saying goodbye was necessary. I didn't say goodbye when I moved to the U.S. The ceremony was very important.

At the end of the session, I decided to go back to China for a farewell party for the team, the clients, and my family. I booked the flight tickets in December, before Christmas. I wanted to spend Christmas and New Year in the U.S.

Finally, on June 24th, Mike and I drove to Chicago. In the car, I practiced my two presentations with Mike. He gave me feedback and corrected the pronunciation of some words.

When we arrived in Chicago, we went to Chinatown. I was keen to have Shaanxi Liangpi (Chinese street food). My tongue remembered the flavor. When I had it, I was not so excited. We thought we missed the food so much from our memory. But the tongue and the sense changed. I did a little research and found some reasons behind this change.

Since we moved to the U.S., our diet has become a mix of Western and Chinese food. Western food may have started reshaping my taste buds.

There's also something called olfactory memory override. I had been using Western herbs like basil and parsley more often, and they might have been dulling my brain's response to familiar

Chinese seasonings—like the spiciness from chili peppers and chili oil or the acidity from aged vinegar. These bold flavors are key to Shaanxi Liangpi, but now they didn't feel as sharp or exciting to me.

Another reason could be the immigrant identity shift. Subconsciously, immigrants may downplay old tastes to adapt more quickly to a new culture. I felt this myself. I learned to cook Western food because I wanted to embrace the new culture. The food from my old culture didn't seem to match my new identity very well anymore.

I also visited a Chinese grocery store next to the library called Park to Shop, where I fundraised in 2014 during my volunteer program. I stood at the front and asked for donations to support our team going to Africa. Many Asian people were generous, and I even remember one woman from Hong Kong who went back to her car to get the cash for a donation.

How time flies.

We drove to the airport to collect Xiaoyun and Lin Zeng. Lin Zeng arrived earlier, and when we met, we hugged and cried. It had been quite a long time since we had last met. When I met Xiaoyun, she greeted me with quiet calmness.

We booked an Airbnb house in the Ukrainian Village neighborhood. Ping Ni, who attended my training program a few years ago, came to Chicago for a business trip with her coworker.

We chose a Ukrainian restaurant called Tryzub Kitchen for our get-together. We supported a Ukrainian business. It was so emotional to meet Ping Ni. Because of the pandemic, we did not have time to meet. She bought gifts for everyone. The food was great. This was my first time eating Ukrainian food. Every meal we ordered was a full portion. I felt the Ukrainians were so generous.

When we went to the restroom, we found a picture of Putin

on the floor, right at the entrance to the restroom. Everyone stamped on him when they went to the restroom. This was the Ukrainian people's way of showing their emotions. We were happy to stamp on the pictures as well.

After the food, Ping Ni came to our Airbnb house to chat. While we were engaged in a lively conversation, her coworker reminded her several times that it was getting late and time to leave. It was only after repeated reminders that she reluctantly said goodbye.

When she left, she found she had forgotten one of her packages, a gift for her family. Lin Zeng promised she would bring the gift to China and meet her somewhere. Meeting outside of China was a special moment for us. As Chinese women and coaches, we felt so connected.

The next day, the conference officially began, and I was excited to see familiar faces. Courtney hosted a private practice constituency meeting. I first met her in 2022 at the NCDA conference, and afterward, I attended her monthly Tuesday Talk sessions. I took part in them for nearly a year, and they provided great professional support. Sometimes, when other coaches had difficulty understanding me, Courtney would summarize my points to help clarify them for the group. She always listened carefully, which I truly appreciated.

Here, I met another coach, Hsiulan Shelley Tien, from Taiwan. We first met at the 2016 NCDA conference in Chicago when she was a board member of the NCDA. She was incredibly kind, inviting the three of us to the international welcome party and taking the time to introduce us to other coaches. Thanks to her, we had more opportunities to connect and expand our network.

For my presentation, "Empowering Women to Overcome Their Imposter Syndrome," more people attended. During this session, I interacted with my audience a lot. They asked me questions during the session, and I answered them very well. The more you practice it, the easier public speaking becomes.

Coach Diane, whom I met at last year's conference, also came to my presentation. We had danced together last year, and after the session, we talked about how coaching flow is like dance. Then I danced with her again to show the flow.

One African American female coach who worked with teenage girls came to me to discuss how to organize a workshop about role models to inspire African American girls. I thought that it was a great way to inspire girls. If they had powerful women as role models, they would become more confident and powerful.

For my round table, I shared "Using Mantras to Move Clients from Insecurity to Confidence." Xiaoyun helped me take pictures. Keri also had her round table next to me, but she didn't have any help. I asked Xiaoyun to take some pictures of Keri. Women support women.

During the session, I taught the audience to write their mantras. At the end of this session, a career coach who was the director of the career center at a famous university talked to me. She said her university students needed this. They were top university students, and they still did not think they were great. They could write their new mantras to practice. Later, she wrote on her LinkedIn profile that my roundtable was one of her most impressive presentations.

My favorite part was Dance Night. This was the happiest time. The three of us made a playful video, then we jumped into the dance. It was a kind of exercise to release all the stress. With music and dim lighting, I could be with my body and express myself with different postures. During the dance, I forgot others and was just in my world. Even though I never learned to dance, I could move naturally. Everybody can do it.

Xiaoyun and I went to a restaurant to talk about the business. She oversaw the Basic Training Program, and only six people joined. I asked Xiaoyun,

"Do you want to continue?"

She said, "No, we can stop!"

I agreed with her, and that was what I wanted. I told Xiaoyun we would cease all business and that I would be returning to China in December for a farewell party to conclude everything.

After this conference, we drove to Michigan. On the way, we stopped at a nice place called Calumet Fisheries to have smoked fish. I learned about this restaurant from Anthony Bourdain's "No Reservations." In that documentary, Antony bought some fish and sat by the roadside to eat it. We were lucky to get the only table just as one couple finished their food. When we had the fish, we saw the bridge lift, and one guy ran to his car, which was parked on the bridge, to drive away. A large ship passed through as the bridge opened. It was lucky the driver moved his car away.

We planned to visit One World Center, where I did my volunteering program. But it was temporarily closed, and we could not stay there. We got another Airbnb house in South Bend. It was an old house built in the 1950s. All the windows were closed, and the alarm was there.

One morning, Xiaoyun fried the eggs, and the smoke was very strong because we could not open the windows. The alarm went off, and I turned it off immediately. When we were having breakfast, we heard a firetruck alarm approaching. I was thinking about a house in the neighborhood that might have caught fire.

The truck finally stopped in front of our house, and we watched from the windows as two police officers came to our house.

The fire truck was for us!

The alarm system was directly connected to the fire department. Mike explained what had happened. The police officers smiled, told us to have a good day, and then left. We teased Xiaoyun:

"Your two fried eggs brought a fire truck and police officers, and you will never forget the U.S.!"

We drove to One World Center. We were surprised that the two girls who took care of the building were there. They let us go inside to walk around. Mike saw his office and his desk. A lot of memories here. In 2022, when we revisited the site, there were few volunteers. The pandemic hit it badly, and it was on the edge of closing.

I appreciated this place for giving me such a unique experience. That volunteer program changed the course of my life. It opened my eyes to the world and gave me the chance to work with people from diverse backgrounds, planting the seed for my passion to support them. It was also where I met Mike, which eventually led me to immigrate to the U.S. Many of my clients wanted to do this program, but they didn't make it. I think every choice has a risk. Trust your heart; you won't get lost. Your heart will bring you to the place where you want to go.

One of my clients once told me something she read in a book that really inspired her:

"The best time to make a change was ten years ago. The second-best time is now."

Chicago Trip

I thanked myself for taking action ten years ago.
If you didn't do it ten years ago, do it now!

Chapter 22
Getting an Offer

After the Chicago trip, we headed to the UK on July 17th. Mike's father, John, got worse, and he went to be looked after in a care home.

When we arrived at the Woodbridge train station, Anne and her lovely dog Sammy met us there. Anne was very stressed as she felt very guilty about putting John there. But she could not take care of him by herself. They were both in their eighties.

In the morning, we planned to visit John, the care home called Anne. John had a cough and fever, so the ambulance came to take him to the hospital. We had to delay our visit. Anne visited John there a few times.

A few days later, when the doctor moved John to the inpatient department, we finally visited him. He sat there with other old, sick men around him. He could recognize us, but he could not say anything to us. His skin was covered in bruises, and he had lost more weight. He tried to smile to liven us up.

I felt so sad, and I could not stop my tears. When my father and uncles were sick, I was not there. This was my first time visiting an old male relative in the hospital. He was so weak and blocked in his world, and no one could understand him.

After one week, John went back to the care home, and we visited him again. He always mentioned he wanted to go home, and Anne tried to comfort him like a mother to a child. Anne was very frustrated, and John was very emotional.

I held his arm and helped him sit in a quiet place. When the nurse came, I was surprised John noticed her. He tried to say hi to her, but the words were stuck between his teeth. It took a lot of effort for the words to escape from his lips, and when they did, they came out stutteringly. I could not reply. I just looked at him and listened to him. I could feel his emotions. He felt stressed. For a while, John stopped talking and became quiet. Maybe he was tired, or he released a little emotion.

We both sat there silently.

At night, Mike and I spent time listening to Anne. She carried so much on her shoulders, sharing the weight of her suffering as a devoted partner to someone with Alzheimer's disease.

"You have your husband, but you can't truly communicate with him. It's like he's physically here, but his soul is gone."

Her words hit me deeply. I had never seen Alzheimer's through the eyes of a spouse before.

Anne also spoke about her identity crisis. She had been a housewife for decades, dedicating herself to supporting John. Her identity had been deeply intertwined with his, and now that he was in elder care, a part of her felt lost.

For women of Anne's generation, family always came first. Every time we visited the UK, she took charge—planning everything and cooking wonderful meals. She was a strong and independent Western woman, yet she sacrificed so much to support John in his successful career as a diabetes specialist.

She thanked us for listening. Just being able to speak her truth made her feel a little lighter.

This time, we took another self-guided trip to the west of England. We chose to travel by train, which took us through Oxford, Plymouth, and Penzance, passing beautiful countryside and running along the sea. We arrived at Land's End, the westernmost point of mainland England.

That slow train journey often comes to my mind, and makes me pause and reflect on how different my life has become. It has become a new life metaphor for me: riding a slow train, passing through the countryside and along the shore, watching birds and people on the beach, admiring colorful landscapes and brilliant family gardens. When the train stops, I step out and go shopping, explore, talk to people, and play on the beach. There is time to pause and take it all in.

My previous life felt more like a crowded underground subway—I was only focused on getting to the next station, pushing through the crowd to escape.

On our last day, we met Mike's uncle, who was eighty-four years old, older than John, and living in London. To better understand the inner world of a British elderly man, I planned a video interview.

I had mailed him all the questions ahead of time since he didn't use email. He had lived his entire life as a single man, working as an English teacher. He had no TV, no internet, no computer, just a simple phone without internet access. Instead, he spent his time reading. He told us he had finished more than two hundred books during the pandemic.

He was dressed sharply in a suit, a long-sleeved shirt, and a black hat when we met him in London. I have a vivid memory that still lingers with me. One evening, when the family gathered at a bar, it started raining as we stepped outside. While the rest of us rushed home, he walked calmly in the rain with his long jacket, black hat, and walking stick. That scene stayed with me—he embodied the elegance and composure of a true English gentleman, like something out of an old movie.

He was so happy to see us, full of energy and speaking clearly. From him, I realized everyone has their own way of living, and we don't all have to follow the traditional path of marriage and children. If you want to be single, just be single.

We chose a quiet park for the interview. My questions covered his daily life, aging and health, being single, relationships with women, family history, death, culture, and religion. He had prepared well, even writing all his answers in a notebook. Mike hosted the interview while I worked as the camerawoman.

Afterward, we invited him to lunch at Din Tai Fung, a well-known Chinese restaurant, and later, we went to a bar. He told us that when King Charles married Diana, he had watched it on TV in this very bar. Time changes everything, but memories stay fresh.

Every time I travel to the UK, I find strength and a sense of relaxation that help me move forward.

Before I came back to the U.S., I got an interview email from Almund Health. I was confused when I sent my resume to this company. I searched for it, and I found it in May. When I was ready for the job, this company replied. It was the right time.

After I came back, I had two interviews in August with the same recruiter from Almund Health. The interview went smoothly, and I got an offer on August 17th. This was a contract job, and my role was life and well-being coach. The recruiter told me the clients were employees of American corporations. They had many work and life issues. The co-founder and CEO was an Asian woman. This was what I was looking for, and I made it.

Now, Almund Health is a leading global mental health solution. Its rapid growth is closely linked to the mental health crisis that intensified during the pandemic. The pandemic pushed me to stop and also created a new opportunity for me.

It felt surprisingly easy, and I had completed my job search. Over the past few years, I had built on my easy and joyful pattern to replace my hard work pattern. So, I made things much easier.

The onboarding process took me more than one month. I needed to take an online training journey and wait for the kickoff call. I felt like a part of American culture, being independent and trusted. You do it by yourself, and you are trusted to accomplish your goal.

During this period, I was very stressed. One day, I sat on the mat to go inward and see my emotions. My worries surfaced:

"Will American clients accept me? Will American corporations treat me well?"

Then I saw Chinese mountains and rivers coming to my mind. I asked them:

"Hi, mountains and rivers. Can you tell me how to deal with it?"

Silence.

I heard a voice:

"Don't worry! American mountains and rivers will embrace you. We are one."

I turned to American mountains and rivers, and I asked them the same question:

"Hi, mountains and rivers. Can you tell me how to deal with it?"

Again, I heard a voice:

"Don't worry! American people are friendly and nice, and they will support you. We are one."

My tears ran out of my eyes, and I released all the stress. I felt nature surrounded me, and it hugged me.

Yes, we are one; the Chinese mountains and rivers and the American mountains and rivers are one. Chinese people and American people are one. We are all human beings and live on one Earth. We support each other.

I knew I was always being supported by people, by nature, by the universe.

The American people, corporations, and the workplace would be the setting for the next phase of my experience. This was a new playground, and my new journey was about to begin.

Chapter 23
ICF Converge

I learned about ICF Converge 2023 from Hellen when she passionately asked me if I was interested in attending. ICF Converge is hosted by ICF every two years. Coaches from all over the world gather to share, learn, and connect. It is similar to the NCDA conference.

Hellen and I had never met in person, even though she had been my coach since 2020, and I had never been to an ICF conference before. On August 23rd, 2023, we finally met at Orlando Airport. When I hugged her, my tears came. On the way to the hotel, Hellen suggested that we stop at a Chinese restaurant to get some food. Even though she had been living in the Western world for over twenty years, Chinese food was still her favorite.

In the Uber, Hellen asked the driver which Chinese restaurant was good. The driver was an African American man, and he was very kind. He recommended a restaurant, drove us there, and waited outside while we got food and brought it back to the hotel.

In the following days, we stayed up chatting until nearly 1 a.m. I felt like I was back in college. One night, we talked about language learning. Hellen shared with me that she had came to

Canada in her early twenties. She trained her brain to think in English first, and she intentionally designed her environment by choosing to surround herself with English-speaking communities and workplaces. She fully immersed herself in this environment, and now her English is like her native tongue.

Over time, Hellen gradually picked up her Chinese again because she wanted to communicate with her family on a deeper level and to support Chinese coaches to become their version of master coaches. Such meaningful motivation helped her relearn Chinese. When we met at the airport, I spoke Chinese to her. I trusted her to communicate back with me in Chinese, and she did exactly what I had trusted. She responded to me in Chinese very well.

Her experience helped me understand more about how to train my brain to learn English. I knew many Chinese immigrants who had come to the U.S. in their twenties. Some still spoke reasonable Chinese, though not as fluently. Some spoke Chinese well, but their English remained so-so.

From my observation, people with higher education in China often found it more difficult to improve their speaking and listening in English than those who did not receive higher education.

New research has shown that the language center for Chinese is closely connected to the brain's motor area. Learning Chinese often relies on physical actions like reading, writing, and speaking to build memory. In contrast, learning English works better when we create a phonetic environment and focus on listening and speaking, since the English language center is closer to the brain's auditory area.

Most Chinese students who make it to university are visual learners. But auditory and kinesthetic learners often don't fit well in China's current education system. Visual learners tend to rely on written words, which can make it harder to build English thinking. They may look at the text first or think of the spelling before understanding the meaning, creating a pattern of "sound → written form → meaning."

Take me for example. I am a strong visual learner. When I see a new English word, I need to remember its spelling first before I can think of the sound. But quick learners often go straight to the sound and remember it that way. My approach makes it harder to pronounce new words quickly.

I can see from Hellen's case that training the brain is a good way to learn a language. I realized I could create change from within my subconscious. When she gave me a short coaching session about English study, I saw a beautiful white girl with long brown hair and a nice white dress dancing around me. Inside my heart, there lived an old Chinese woman. I loved the white girl, but she could not come into my heart.

I realized that, on the one hand, I wanted to improve my English, but in my subconscious, I rejected English. Consciously, I knew that if I had good English, it would be great for my life and career in the U.S. Subconsciously, I sensed that English symbolized cultural betrayal. I deeply love the Chinese language. Through it, I read many books to understand the world, and I also like to write. Since elementary school, I have been journaling. I have twenty to thirty notebooks written in Chinese. I wanted to be a writer when I was young and, of course, I meant a Chinese writer.

I think generally many Chinese men have stronger feelings of cultural betrayal than women, as men have a strong sense of territory. But I have more connection with language than most people. The Chinese language was my love, like my mom. I could not let her go to accept English. I was struggling because of the inner resistance.

Then I tried to talk to the Chinese lady, and she agreed that she could leave. We both cried. She knew I would have a new life. She could support me in other ways. When the Chinese woman left, the white girl came to the center of my heart, but she was so weak that she could not stand up. She had to curl up to sleep.

During the conference, miraculous things happened. I attended one presentation, but I didn't like it, so I went out. Just then, I saw Hellen coming out of her presentation, and she had done the same thing.

We had gone to the same session but sat in different rows. I chose a seat next to a woman in the front row and noticed she was using a tree map to take notes. We had a quick conversation. Her name was Grace, and she was from Canada.

Before the presentation ended, I stepped out early for the restroom. While washing my hands, I ran into Grace again. I noticed her necklace and said,

"I feel you are the soil that cultivates other plants."

She was thrilled to hear that.

When I walked outside, I saw a coach in a green suit. It was Moon, a Chinese coach from the UK who had just received the 2023 ICF Coaching Impact Award. I stopped her and started a conversation. Moon told me she lived in the UK because her husband was British. I mentioned that I had just come back from the UK, and we instantly felt closer.

Moon also shared that she was trained at Co-Active, and I told her that Hellen was as well. Just then, Hellen arrived and joined our conversation. The two of them were so happy to meet each other.

At that moment, Grace also came outside and joined us. The four of us stood there, chatting enthusiastically outside the restroom. It was a moment of pure connection, an energy miracle. We even took pictures to capture the magic of that moment.

During the sessions, I tried to connect with people, not just through words, but through energy and heart. At night, Hellen and I talked about who had good energy. She shared a story about an encounter she had with another MCC.

She once entered a meeting room and chose an empty seat. Next to it was a notebook, but no one was there. Later, a man arrived. He paused, looked around, and said,

"Who moved my stuff?"

Hellen was shocked because no one had touched anything. Then she noticed his name tag—it said MCC. His first words were full of judgment and created pressure in the room.

MCC is not just a credential but a state of mastery, a flowing and living state of being. This story made me realize that I don't need to rush to pursue an MCC credential. I need to live the MCC mood: open, spacious, wise, and slow. I needed to give myself and others space, to hold others and myself with no judgment.

At the end of the conference, another keynote speaker shared the crazy things he had tried. He asked everybody to write a bucket list. I had an immediate idea: to hug the tall men to feel a connection in this big meeting room.

My male family members, my husband, and I were not tall, and I was very curious about tall men. I noticed a man sitting alone, deeply focused on his writing. I remembered Toni mentioning that he was the tallest man at the conference.

Curiously, I walked over and asked for his permission. He gave me a hug, bending his body. It was difficult to reach his shoulder, and this hug was not very comfortable. I felt he was not happy and was a little closed.

I went to another tall man, who was happy at that moment with the other coaches. When we hugged, I could feel the openness, acceptance, energy, and passion. It was completely different. That moment showed me that our energy shapes connection more than physical presence. Because of his energy, I also gave back my power and passion. One can affect others immediately.

From that experience, I felt a deeper connection with my body. You can feel energy and connection from a single hug.

I had a great time at this conference. I also learned that being playful was very important for a coach. On our way back to the airport, we had lunch again at the same Chinese restaurant. It seemed Hellen's brain was well-trained for Chinese food, not Western food!

When I came back from this conference, I wrote in my diary in English. Also, I translated my daily mantras into English, and I read them in English every day. I also read over twenty English books. This was why I felt very comfortable and brave enough to write this book, my first in English.

During the conference, I met Toni many times. When we went to the restroom together, she mentioned that I should join ICF Charlotte as a board member. I had never thought about it, but I was interested in this new experience as I had never been a board member.

Later, I found one coach I met in May who became a board member of ICF Charlotte, and it inspired me. I contacted Toni, and we had a nice ride along the Greenway and a great meal at a German restaurant. After I submitted my application, I was accepted as the Director of Events on the ICF Charlotte board.

The Power of Resourcefulness

It went so smoothly!

Chapter 24
A Black Kitten

When I came back from ICF Converge, I watched a movie called *Coraline*. I was so fond of this movie. It was the story of a girl who moved to an apartment with her parents. There was a hidden door in the dining room. Coraline met a boy who was the grandson of the owner, and he also brought a black cat. She went through the door in the dining room in her dream, and the cat followed her. She had a pleasant experience.

There was another mother and father. They treated her so well and supplied her with delicious food, nice clothing, a magical garden, and fun performances and shows. They always asked her what she wanted and tried to fulfill her wishes.

The other mother, a spider, trapped her and wanted to sew buttons over her eyes when she returned one day. She escaped, but this evil spider kidnapped her real parents. She had to go back to fight this evil spider. The black cat and the boy helped her rescue her parents and defeat it.

Coraline's fashionable style and her bravery attracted me, especially with that wise black cat.

. . .

On August 31st, during my following coaching session, I explored my new second life in the U.S. I was going to start my career in the U.S., and it was a new beginning. During this session, I created vivid pictures:

It was another Coraline sitting outside the apartment and reading a book. A dog and a black cat surrounded her. Coraline wanted to explore the world. She carried her bag and brought her black kitten into her bag to leave the house.

When I described the pictures to Hellen, she asked me if I'd like to try something different—to stand up, find a bag, and then find another object that could represent my black cat. I found my bag in the cupboard and put it on my shoulder. I used my cell phone to represent the black cat and placed it in the bag. After that I walked around the room, pretending to explore the world.

Eventually, I stopped, closed my eyes, and created my new pictures: Coraline went to an old mansion with an enormous garden, like King Charles's garden. The owner was a woman. Coraline got a job as a gardener. There was an old gardener who guided her.

Coraline took care of many flowers, and her black cat helped her. During the night, Coraline and her cat chose fresh flowers to sleep in. Coraline chose a big one, and her cat chose a small one. Coraline also took care of some green plants without flowers.

People knew there was a magic garden in this place. The garden was sometimes open to the public. The landlady, a strong, kind, spiritual woman, always wore long dresses. The old gardener was wise, and he taught Coraline a lot.

With Coraline and her cat's care, the flowers were blooming, and they liked Coraline. When Coraline and her cat walked among the flowers, the flowers said hi to them, smiled at them, and even gently touched them with their leaves and branches to show their love.

Such a beautiful picture!

Hellen curiously asked me,

"Who are the flowers?"

"The women," I said.

Yes, in my American career, I would continue to support women. The green plants meant men. I also would support men, but they were not my majority.

Hellen stayed very present with me and followed with another question,

"Who is the old gardener?"

I thought for a moment, then said,

"He represents ordinary people I've met in my life. They have life wisdom, and while getting along with them, I learn a lot."

When I talked about the old gardener, another picture flashed in my mind.

The landlady invited Coraline, her cat, and the old gardener to afternoon tea. They sat in the garden and enjoyed the tea. It was so great. Coraline liked her landlady, who wore a long dress. When Coraline grew up, she became the landlady. The landlady was an adult Coraline!

From this session, I understood my new journey in the U.S. was to support women, similar to what I did in China. Finally, I became the landlady who owned the mansion and the garden, who was powerful, wise, and kind. I would build my business and kingdom to do this. The black cat was my enormous support.

This session brought my black kitten, Happy, into my life.

I was reading the book *Cleo: How a Small Black Cat Helped Heal a Family* by Helen Brown. When I saw this book in a second-hand store in Woodbridge in the UK, the cute cover of a black kitten attracted me to it. I bought it immediately and brought it to the U.S. It was a long story, and I read it slowly.

One day, when I read the emotional part, I felt tears. I thought I might adopt a black kitten now. I immediately went to the Petfinder website. A black kitten, Sabrina, instantly attracted me. She was so curious and cute in her eyes, and I fell in love with her.

Then, I contacted the animal shelter. The staff member replied the cat was available, and she sent me an application form. When I volunteered at the animal shelter, there were many black cats for adoption as the culture regards black cats as having no good luck.

I didn't fill out the form right away as I felt very blocked in my stomach. I talked to Mike, and he said one cat was good. Since Hope died in July 2022, Freedom was the only cat in our house. He became closer to us, and he got all the attention. Sometimes, I felt he was lonely, especially when we traveled outside the U.S. We wanted to adopt one more to accompany him.

In May, we went to an animal shelter and found a young black cat. When we went back to adopt it, we found out that the shelter had given it to another family. We felt furious, and then I realized we had not been ready. The thought of more responsibility and death frightened us. Hope's death made us feel so bad. I felt very guilty and blamed myself for not taking care of her very well.

The blocked part of my stomach was the emotion of fear. Then, I made a conscious choice to face my fear and open myself to love. To love needs bravery, I told myself. I wrote my name on the form and became the person responsible for taking care of this cat.

I asked Hellen to write a reference letter, and I sent the form back to the staff. The staff member said it was no problem, but she was at the beach for a vacation and would come back in a few days. When she contacted me again, she said we might pick the kitten up on September 9th as she would come back from vacation that day. It was our wedding anniversary. I agreed with her.

She came back on the afternoon of September 9th. When I got the notice, we drove there to pick up the kitten. Before we reached the shelter, I was very nervous. It was like picking a child.

Sabrina was with her other four siblings, three girls and one boy. They were all black with collars of different colors. I recognized her and petted her. She wasn't shy and seemed to enjoy being petted.

After completing the adoption process, we placed her in the cat carrier and set it on the back seat. I sat next to her. She did not even cry. On the way, I opened the cage a little, and she went outside to explore the seat and then sat quietly on my leg.

From then on, she became our sweet daughter and brought so much joy and many lessons to me. We changed her name from Sabrina to Happy as we wanted to be happy. Happy became the greatest gift for our seventh wedding anniversary.

Happy came to my house when I started my American career. When I introduced myself to my clients, I mentioned I had two cats. One was called Freedom, and the other was called Happy. They felt very interested.

Sometimes, Happy would lie on top of my chair's backrest, visible to my clients through the camera. Other times, she would sit right in front of the camera, stealing all the attention. Sometimes, she would jump onto my lap and sleep there for hours during my coaching sessions. She was an incredible source of support on this journey, offering emotional comfort and companionship. I turned my visualization into reality.

Happy became Coraline's wise black cat.

Chapter 25
A New Journey

When my bio was shown on the Almund Health platform at the end of September, I was very nervous. Who would come to me?

In the first two days, there were no clients. On the third day, October 2nd, I had an appointment with a Chinese American man and a white woman. Soon, diverse clients came to me: Asian immigrants (first and second generation), African American, Latino, and white men, and first-generation African and European immigrants.

This coaching job opened the door for me to experience American professional life. For the first month, I did not have many clients, and then for the second month, in November, my calendar was fully booked. I needed to coach them in Chinese and English.

I found that speaking two languages helped me attract more clients. I printed the most common English questions and read them aloud. It gave me more confidence to ask English questions.

When I was receiving my coaching training, although our trainers were Canadian, our clients were Chinese. We practiced asking questions in Chinese. When asking English questions, I needed to prepare for them. I still felt overwhelmed. Hellen was traveling and spending time with her parents in China, so she was not available to have a session with me or provide immediate support.

One day, when I was in the Zoom meeting waiting for my client, I felt my body shaking and couldn't stop it. This client did not show up, and then I had time to sit on my mat and check what happened to me: fear, stress, and frustration.

During the coaching session, I wanted to know exactly where we were in the process and what questions to ask. But I found it was not possible.

For the English sessions, the clients gave too much information at one time, and I could not absorb it. Sometimes, I understood every word, but I could not understand what the clients meant. I always felt very embarrassed to ask the clients to explain it to me again. I didn't want to appear confused. Losing control during coaching sessions and facing uncertainty made me more stressed.

I tried to coach myself when I calmed down. Then, a picture came to my mind. My client was like a playful child, running freely in a field. I tried very hard to follow her. In the sky, there was a helicopter following us, and the pilot wanted to send me a message based on his judgment.

The client would turn right, and I would prepare to turn right. But the helicopter gradually lost control of the client. I found that I could not get any help. What I could do was to follow the client. When she stopped, I stopped, and when she went to the restroom, I went to the restroom. When she cried, I was with her quietly.

To my surprise, my body stopped shaking, and I felt more peaceful. Following and accompanying the clients instead of trying to lead them made me more relaxed. The clients need to be listened to and seen. They had the resources to solve their own problems. I didn't always need to ask powerful questions. When I found I couldn't control the situation, I accepted myself, and then I released the fear. That was a big step for me. The master of life is the opposite of control.

I had many first-generation immigrant clients, some from Asia, some from Africa, some from Europe, and some from South America. They all had common issues with communication and self-confidence. When we went deep, they always thought their English was not good.

Some had studied in the U.S. for a master's degree or PhD, and some had been in the U.S. for more than ten years, even twenty years. I realized it did not matter how many years you were in the U.S. What mattered was how you saw yourself. The language issue was a common one for immigrants. Behind it was a psychological disadvantage, especially if you were from a developing country and you were not confident.

One of my Asian clients said that when she talked in a meeting, her coworkers did not respond. When her boss repeated what she said, they reacted. She felt so embarrassed and blamed her communication for being poor.

I shared my observation:

"I feel you are very anxious when you talk; it looks like you want to run. During communication, people can feel your energy. If you're stressed and blame yourself, you can't stay calm. The first time, they may not understand you. When you repeat yourself, you speak faster and more anxiously, and your coworkers may feel more pressure."

My observation gave her a little awakening. She thought she had a communication problem, but in fact, she was too anxious and wanted everything done fast. She was too eager to be success-ful, and people felt very pressured by her.

One African immigrant client said that during a meeting, she shared an idea, and no one said anything, but at the end of the session, another person shared the same idea, and the rest praised the idea. She felt very hurt and felt that others had ignored her. At the next meeting, she said nothing. She felt very distant from her American coworkers.

I had a similar experience when I worked in the "Fighting with the Poor" volunteer program. At first I was very angry and later I found the reason. When team members didn't really under-stand what I said, they wanted to be polite and didn't interrupt me. Sometimes, I did the same thing to others.

I shared this story with her and then said:

"From my experience, I want to share some thoughts about what happened to you. Your coworker may not have been paying close attention, or maybe you weren't very clear and people didn't fully get it. At the end of meetings, people often just want to finish on time. They try to reach an outcome, so they might pay more attention to the person who spoke last and agree with them. That doesn't necessarily mean they were ignoring you. What do you think of that perspective?"

She paused for a moment and said:

"When it happened, all the voices rushed into my head: 'You're from another country. You don't belong here. They don't pay attention to you.' And then I felt hurt."

Most immigrants carry limiting beliefs and worries about being in a new country: I'm not good enough to be here; I don't feel safe; local people won't treat me well. When something happens, it's easy to trigger those fears.

Then she asked me,

"So how did you deal with it?"

"I just repeated what I said until people understood," I answered.

We both laughed.

At the end of the session, when I asked her about a small action she could take, she mentioned that she might ask her coworkers directly—why they didn't react to what she said—and find out the real reason.

She felt much better after we explored it together.

Another Asian immigrant client who had been in the U.S. for ten years came to me. She had come to the U.S. in her twenties. Her English was great. She spoke English clearly and chose her words very carefully. In one session, she mentioned that she often ate a lot after work, even though she didn't feel hungry. I asked:

"If your mouth can talk, what message does your mouth want to tell you?"

She was quiet for a little while. Then she answered,

"I don't speak all day, and my mouth wants some exercise."

She worked as a software engineer and sat in front of the computer all day. She did not need to talk.

I asked:

"If you give your mouth an opportunity every day, let it talk or even sing, what would happen?"

She said:

"My English is not good, and I don't want to sing and talk!"

I was so shocked, but I understood. I never wanted to listen to my English recordings. I thought my English was not very good before. Most people didn't like their voices.

She asked me how I dealt with this problem, and I shared the tips I learned from the keynote speaker, Dana Sander, at ICF Converge. Dana Sander is the *New York Times* bestselling author of *All In Startup*. In her speech, she mentioned,

"Do not ask 'Is this a yes or no.' Ask 'Is this a 1-10' instead."

Don't say your English is good or bad. You could say that on a scale of 1-10 points, my English is a 5, 6, 7, 8, or 9. I could say my English was 7. For me, 10 was a native speaker who had a high education and could write great articles. I could write, read, and have conversations, even deeply. I could handle my coaching conversations. Every year, my English was improving. It was on the way to 8, then 9, then 10.

Finally, I found I had solved the language issue because of my acceptance of the situation and my surrender. I accepted myself and stopped blaming myself for not having perfect English.

Also, I tried a new strategy: speaking English clearly and slowly. I found that speaking slowly was most important. I gave my clients and myself time. During slow speaking, I showed very calm energy, which made the clients more relaxed. Sometimes, some people could not understand me, but they did not feel nervous.

Many professional immigrants came to the U.S. and gave up their previous jobs to do blue-collar work as drivers, carpenters, receptionists, or housekeepers, as they thought their language was not good enough. The key was not to try to improve your language immediately to level 10, like a native speaker. It was not possible. Rather, it was wise to accept where you were and that you might not make small talk with Americans, as you cannot understand them right now. Instead, focus on what you can improve in a short time—English in your professional area. During the work, you can still improve your English.

This is a growth mindset, not a fixed mindset.

During the first few months, I felt the differences and similarities with clients from different backgrounds:

1. Asian people (men and women) usually had high expecta-

tions of themselves. Women criticized themselves a lot if something happened. They had high stress levels, and they found it hard to express their emotions. They had a lot of struggles within.

2. White women were very independent, but some had a lot of stress and were easily affected by what was going on outside. They usually ignored their emotions of stress and sadness. Some white women I coached tended to appear strong on the outside, and sometimes, it took time to open their hearts to show their weakness. They had a stronger sense of self.

3. African Americans and Latinos had open hearts, were loving, and cared about others, but they lost their energy as they opened their hearts easily, and it was easy to get hurt. They did not spend more time with themselves, and instead, they focused on others. It was easy to connect with their bodies and release their emotions.

There were many clients I had a very vivid memory of, like a middle-aged white woman who was a middle-level manager and suffered from high blood pressure and body pain. Her brain was thinking too much and could not stop. She had the same thought I had before: If you were successful, you would be happy. Now, she was very successful, but the result was health issues and more stress.

She wondered what happiness was. She thought that because I was from China, I naturally knew how to be happy. I told her I wasn't born knowing how to be happy, but I learned about happiness through experiences. During the coaching session, I let her experience slowing down to build her own space to be with herself, not her work.

I experienced self-care from an African American. During one session, she was preparing salad when we started. I gave her time to eat her salad. She enjoyed her salad on the sofa, and I closed my eyes to meditate when the Zoom was on. We enjoyed taking the moment to take care of ourselves, to slow down the pace. After five minutes, when she finished her food, we started our coaching conversation.

I noticed how the first-generation immigrant affected the second-generation immigrant. A second-generation Asian immigrant girl mentioned she didn't spend her money because she felt guilty. During the session, I asked her to use a metaphor for money. She chose a glass vase—something easy to break—to represent it.

When she spoke about her father, emotion overcame her and she began to weep. Her father was the eldest child in a poor family from East Asia. He tried to take care of the whole family and worked very hard. When he immigrated to the U.S., he tried to save every penny and often told the rest of the family: don't waste money. When she grew up, she did not dare spend any money on her own. After she had released all her emotions, she felt she deserved to spend her own money.

I learned that time did not change one's connection with their birth country. A Latina woman's family moved to the U.S. when she was in middle school. Even after having a baby, she still felt that her birth country, which is a small country on the western coast of South America, was truly her home. She didn't feel very connected to her adopted country.

Anyway, they generally had a stronger spirit than my previous female clients in China, but they weren't as confident as I had imagined. Many white female clients came to me because they struggled with imposter syndrome. Some African American clients told me they felt invisible, and a few Asian women mentioned that too—but no white women ever said that. Some Asian women believed that, because they were both minorities and women, they didn't get promoted.

. . .

Usually, I asked my clients: "Why did you choose me as your coach?"

The answers were very rich:

"Your bio picture is impressive: joyful and smiling."

"You are accomplished, and you have done many things and had many experiences."

"You have more certifications (PCC, not ACC) and CMCS."

"You have entrepreneur experience."

"You have diverse experience."

"Your presentation was about imposter syndrome."

"You are a career coach, and I have career issues."

"You were not born in the U.S., and I don't want a coach from the U.S."

"You are an immigrant, and you know my suffering as an immigrant."

"You come from a different culture than mainstream American culture. You might help me think outside the cultural box."

Because of my transition journey, I knew all the deep problems they were suffering as I had had the same experience. I told Hellen that I was able to help my clients not just because of my training but because I had worked through similar issues myself. When I can help myself, I'm better able to help them too. I see myself as resourceful on this journey, and I also trust that others can solve their own problems.

One of the five foundational principles of coaching is that everyone has the resources to solve their own problems. I fully understand resourcefulness now.

Chapter 26
Saying Goodbye to China

On December 6th, 2023, Mike and I went back to China. I had been away from China for nearly four years, since January 2020. The goal was obvious: say farewell to family members and team members. We didn't have a farewell party for the family in 2019, but we arranged it this time. For the team, we planned a big get-together and invited clients and trainees. It was our last get-together.

We visited my mother first in my hometown. Two of my siblings lived nearby. When I met my young brother, eldest sister, and mother, I could not stop my tears.

My young brother had gained a lot of white hair. He quit his job and started his small business, and he had a son during the pandemic. His wife had to quit her job to take care of the baby, and all the economic burdens came onto his shoulders.

My father quit his job at a public hospital when he was in his forties to start his own clinic. He always wanted to have freedom. His entrepreneurial spirit affected me and my brother. I started my business when I was thirty-six, and my brother was forty years old when he started his own business. This is connected with the

Family Career Tree Theory, which explores how family dynamics, values, and experiences shape an individual's career decisions and trajectories over generations.

When we stayed at his house, he stayed up very late working online to grow his business. In him, I saw myself when I started my business: very anxious, with no boundaries between life and work. I met my pandemic nephew. He was energetic and liked to play games, but he got sick very often. They knew it was a COVID-19 variant.

While other siblings had gotten older and had more white hair, my sister-in-law looked very good. Her face was full of vibrant energy. As a stay-at-home mother, she played with her son and brought him to travel nearby, as my brother was very busy. She and her son shared a strong bond and joyful energy.

My mother was in her seventies. After my father passed away, she went to a Christian church very often. She had a good social life and connected with other elderly women like her. She did not want to travel to the U.S. I thought we had very few chances to meet each other. I prepared questions for her and then recorded her answers.

Also, she liked to sing many revolutionary and church songs. She mentioned that before the Cultural Revolution, she had been very popular in school as she sang beautiful songs. As a Red Guard and middle school student during the Cultural Revolution, she took part in student networking events and visited many cities in China. As long as she brought her meal ticket, she could eat at canteens in different cities.

She also went to Beijing, where Zhou Enlai met with her and her fellow Red Guards at Tiananmen Gate on behalf of Chairman Mao. My mother was very good at imitation. She often imitated Zhou Enlai's speeches to us.

In my opinion, my mother lacked independent thinking, but

she was very flexible and adaptable to the environment and the time. And she treated other people kindly. She did not like to read books and trusted only the news on TV channels.

I recorded many of her songs, and she told me she believed China would be even greater in the future. As she said it, she raised her fist with conviction.

On the day we left, my brother drove us to the train station, and we stopped by my mother's house. It was a chilly morning, and she took my hands in hers to warm them. Her hands were so warm, yet a little rough from years of housework. I remembered how, when I was young, my hands were always cold, and she would warm them just like this. At this moment, the warmth, the care, and the love of my mother came rushing back. My eyes welled up with tears.

We also visited some relatives I had not seen for a long time. My aunt (my second uncle's wife) and her son. They lived in a small city where I had studied in high school. In their eyes, life was better. My aunt told me because she was 80 years old, she got more money from the government than old people in the 60s.

She had everything, all the vegetables she grew on the side of the road. They were farmers, and when they moved to the city, they also tried to look for open spaces and planted vegetables. Sometimes, urban management removed the vegetables, so they found other public places to plant. I felt more peaceful with them.

My aunt was older than my mother, and she had never received an education. She had a traditional Chinese woman's wisdom. She was easily self-satisfied and able to survive in difficult situations. I didn't see this kind of wisdom in well-educated women. She was more self-accepting than my mother.

My mother always thought she was better than my aunt as she got more education and worked as a teacher. But in terms of life wisdom, my mother did not have more than my aunt. She had a tense relationship with my father before he died and a tense relationship with my brother for most of her lifetime.

My aunt had a very good relationship with her children. I had lunch with her family only twice, but it felt different from my family. They were very loving, not competing and complaining. It was life wisdom one can never learn in school.

I met my elementary classmate who lived in the next neighborhood. Her parents' house had been next to my aunt's old house in a village where my family had lived for a decade. The Wang clan dominated mainly this village. The entire Wang family was connected going back a few generations.

My classmate's family name is Liu, which differs from Wang. Her family was surrounded by the Wang clan, and they felt very powerless. That's part of what it's like to live in a rural area in China. People often build connections through marriage. She married a man who came from the Wang clan.

We were not as excited as we were supposed to be, although we had not seen each other in over two decades. She was an English teacher at a middle school. She mentioned her classroom was identified as the bad classroom where students could not go to a good middle school. The students did not have a passion for learning.

She shared with me she had sacrificed a lot for her elderly brother, who was a farmer. I could imagine that she had saved most of her salary to support her brother. Most Chinese women with brothers often took on the same self-sacrificing roles because of traditional cultural expectations. I could see myself in that role if I did not pursue my life. It was good to meet her.

On the way back, we crossed the city in a taxi. I could not

recognize it from my memory. There are too many tall buildings around and outside the city for many miles. In 1996, there were villages and green farmland. The villages disappeared, and elementary schools decreased as people moved to the cities.

I felt a little sad as all the memories from my childhood were not found in reality. In my life in China, I witnessed the economy booming, and I could feel all the people running fast, including me. It looked like we knew where we were running to, but when we arrived, even with economic success and material comfort, we felt lost, confused, and anxious.

I invited my brother's family and my mother and sister for food. My brother-in-law got the COVID-19 variant and could not show up. When I thanked them, I felt more emotional and had tears. My eldest sister said,

"Don't cry, just be happy!"

She avoided all emotions. Most Chinese people felt ashamed of showing emotion in front of others. But I was okay with it, as I had become very natural in showing my emotions.

My other siblings lived in another province, so Mike and I took a train to visit them. On the way, we stopped at Nanjing train station for a few hours as I needed to meet my niece, who had given birth to a baby at the end of the pandemic.

She shared her suffering with me when she gave birth to a baby. We were sitting together at a coffee shop in the train station. She said all the female relatives pushed her to have a baby, but no one warned her how painful and dangerous it was to give birth. She was preparing for a normal childbirth, but at the last minute, the doctor gave her a cesarean. Her husband could not come inside as pandemic rules were strict. She had to go into the operating room alone. She was so angry and scared. This was an immediate decision, and no one was prepared. She found a piece of hygienic cloth and placed it on the operating table herself, as there hadn't been one there originally. Then she underwent a painful procedure. She wept as she shared her story, and I hugged her with tears in my eyes.

She had told her stories to her cousins. I was proud of her for saying it out loud. It helped many young women know more about what they would face when they chose to give birth to babies. I felt anger and fear still stuck in her body. It could not find a safe exit.

We continued our journey. When we met the other siblings, we stayed at my second sister's house. Her hair turned all white, and she had to use a wig.

My fourth sister had half-white hair. Her family ran a trucking business, which was affected a lot during the pandemic. Her son was in 11th grade. He had asked for leave to have lunch with the family on Saturday, as his entire class had extra lessons on weekends.

Since the pandemic, a new word has emerged in China: 内卷 (involution). It describes how people work harder, such as working overtime or attending extra tutoring, yet gain no real advantage and only experience collective exhaustion. Education has also been affected. My nephew's situation is one example of how involution has affected students.

My nephew's classmates wanted him to ask Mike and me,

"Do you have the guns?"

They thought every person in the U.S. had guns, as there were many shootings on TV news. In their eyes, we lived in a hail of bullets every day.

We answered the question:

"We don't have any guns. We will not buy one in the future!"

My fourth sister invited us for dinner at the restaurant, which was run by my elementary school classmate's family. During the dinner, her husband talked on the phone all the time in order to maintain his business network. He shared that the business was harder than before and that he had to work very hard. Life was too noisy for them. They had phone calls and social media, and did not have their quiet time.

I came to the kitchen to meet my classmate. We had not met since we graduated from middle school (we had studied at the same elementary school and middle school). I could not recognize him from the face, only from the voice.

He mentioned his son was seventeen years old and in high school. As his son did not get enough scores for the high school in this city (the competition was very brutal), the boy was sent to his mother's hometown to study. My classmate and his wife were away from their only son and worked very hard. He said that after the pandemic, the business was not good. He expected a high boost in business, but it did not happen. We did not know what we wanted to talk more about, so we ended the evening.

We visited another aunt, who was my eldest uncle's wife in her eighties. She was ill all the time, so her son rented a simple room on the first floor of his apartment building. There were a few square meters full of a table, cooking stuff, and her bed. There was only a little space next to her bed. Mike, my sister, and I had to go to her one by one.

My aunt was sleeping and she always stayed on her bed. I knew this was the last time I would meet her. I felt very sad to see that she lived in such a messy environment. My uncle died in 2019, and he left money for his children to take care of my aunt. I asked my sister angrily,

"When her son let her live in such an environment, why did you say nothing?"

193

"Her daughter even said nothing! As a niece, what can I say?" my sister said.

I felt so sad for my old aunt.

My sister woke my aunt and introduced me and Mike to her. She recognized me. We hugged and wept. Although we lived very far apart, I remember that when her son got married in the 1980s, she brought me to buy some food. She gave me braised pig's ear to eat on the way back. Her hand that held me was so warm and strong, and the food was so delicious. From then on, I fell in love with braised pig's ear. That tall, strong, and warm-hearted woman now lay on the bed in a small corner in such a big world.

My aunt asked me whether we had children. I told her we did not want a child. She still said,

"It is good to have a child!"

The concept of raising children to protect against old age was too deep in her era, but in my era, it is already very shallow. From her experience, I saw she benefited little from her children in her eighties. She might have had a comfortable and decent living environment if she did not have children.

My mother and two aunts were traditional Chinese women, and they devoted themselves to their children. In Chinese history, there were many women like them who raised, loved, and protected their children from going through tough times. When life became better, they still kept a very frugal lifestyle. For them, mother and wife were their major identities. Most of the time, they forgot themselves.

Every day, it felt like our only job was to eat. At first, our stomachs were happy, but then they became tired and exhausted. My sister's pet turtle lifted my spirits. He has been with my sister's family for more than twenty years. He felt very cold and always looked for a warm place. When I turned on the air conditioning in our bedroom, he always slowly crawled into the room. He usually hid under Mike's dirty clothes on the floor. He did not have a specific name; my sister just called him "Xiao Wu Gui" in Chinese. Mike gave him a new name, Slow Coach. He had more peaceful energy than anyone I had met.

We invited all the family members for lunch at the restaurant to thank them for all their support. When I mentioned we would not come back very often, I realized this was a big separation I had to accept in my life.

From my observation, people who lived in big cities felt more stressed than people who lived in small cities and rural areas. When I took the subway in Shanghai, I felt so tired. The crowded subway drained my energy. Most people were just on their phones on the subway. I met coaches, and some were more anxious.

Finally, the get-together was hosted in Shanghai. The coaches on our team traveled from different cities, and so did some clients. I shared on the topic of career transition and emotional balance. Two of my classmates at the university also came. Mike shared about his working experience in different countries, such as the U.S., the UK, Denmark, China, and Angola. Yali shared about professional topics in the post-pandemic career field.

After the sharing, I asked the team members to the stage. It was our time of separation. I hugged every member. They shared their feelings, and we gave each other blessings. My tears came. I was so emotional. I could feel every hug. Some were very warm and accepting; some were very heavy; some just wanted to put their weight on me. Clients were very shocked, and they did not know this was our last meeting, but this was a farewell.

More people came to the stage, and we hugged and cried. Lin Zeng asked one coach to feel the energy. She said she felt like different river streams that went in different directions. Yes, we would go in different directions in the future. Jing Wang and Lei Guo took our seven WeChat group resources to continue to help women with a new name. I was happy they transcended the spirit to help women.

After the get-together, we went to eat together. More than ten coaches attended this farewell dinner. We tried to play different games. Everyone could choose one person at the table to ask questions. When they talked, other people couldn't disturb them.

Then we went to another game: silence. Everyone was silent. I had time to bring my attention to myself. I felt so tired and couldn't breathe in the room. This restaurant was in the shopping center, so the air was not fresh. I had not gone outside all afternoon and evening. In that time, Xiaoyun closed her eyes, and her face was full of tears. When we hugged, she held back from crying. But now, it was her moment.

I went outside with Yali for some fresh air. There were many small vendors around the shopping center, and the owners were young people. Yali said the consumption went lower, and many people tried to find flexible jobs to make a living. I read similar news while I was in the U.S. After this walk, I went back to the hotel earlier, as the team members would meet tomorrow morning, and I had finished the most important part for today.

In the early morning, I woke up and felt my stomach too full. In those days, I always felt emotions inside, but I could not release them. I got up quietly so as not to wake up Mike and sat on a yoga mat. This time, I focused on my breath and went deep. Many pictures flashed into my mind: the chef classmate's tired and anxious eyes; my sister sharing with me how her mother-in-law suffered from body pain; and one of the career coach's white hairs.

I burst into tears, which woke up Mike. I felt very sad, like a child whose loved ones were suffering. I was sad to leave all the familiar faces and everything I had created.

Mike woke up to hug me. He was always there to support me. I asked him to go to sleep. I needed time to be with myself. Gradually, I felt more peaceful. I mourned my loss.

After breakfast, we agreed that all the coaches would go to one hotel room to chat. In Xin Zhao's room, everybody shared their feelings. This was our last time sharing.

Yali shared first. She talked about her fear of being alone in the future. My body felt so painful. I moved next to Xin Zhao, and she gave me a massage. My shoulders, back, and head were in sharp pain. Hanbin said to me,

"Don't worry, we can take care of ourselves. You let yourself go to pursue your dream!"

Her words moved me to tears, and I realized I was still holding on—like a mother not ready to let go.

When it came to Xiaoyun, she said yesterday during silence time she realized she had emotions to process. She had not recognized it until she was silent.

Xiaoyun mentioned the father's daughter and mother's daughter from the book *The Heroine's Journey* by Maureen Murdock. Father's daughter means that as a woman, you use your brain too much, and you are rational and follow a patriarchal way. Mother's daughter means you connect with your body and emotions. You are more sensitive and loving.

Most of the time, Xiaoyun was the father's daughter. She used her brain too much as she was too close to her father and was far from her mother. She shared the picture that her mother was also watching her from a distance, but she did not see her mother. When she went back to her mother, she became her mother's daughter. She felt she could freely release her emotions and get her strength back, connect with her heart, and feel love.

"I know you worry about me. Now, I am strong. You don't need to worry about me. I can take care of myself very well," Xiaoyun said to me.

I felt a rush of emotion, and tears streamed down my face.

Xiaoyun came to my team in 2020, and most of the time, she was very rational. She shared with her brain, not her heart. In her, I saw another me a long time ago, full of anger and trying to analyze everything in my brain.

Now, her awareness had moved from her rational brain to her emotions and feelings. From what she said, I also knew that the years I connected with my body and my emotions were a kind of process of becoming a mother's daughter. I had been a father's daughter. Now, I am more flexible. Most of the time, I am a mother's daughter, and sometimes I can change to be a father's daughter.

We shared, cried, and hugged. One coach said we were all here because of me, and I realized she was right. I had built this platform. I was so proud of myself at that moment. Everyone was a creator. In 2016, I no longer wanted to work for other people, and I wanted to meet people who had values that were like mine. I created my platform, and more people joined.

I was also proud of being brave enough to let it go. I learned this wisdom: "Where there are gains, there must be losses; where there are losses, there must be gains." My life was a river, and I could not be stuck in one place forever as I would go to the sea.

After a number of hugs and tears, most coaches left before lunch. Several went to lunch. During lunch, Yali said she hadn't realized this was separation until this morning when the coaches left one by one. She was not ready for the separation. She had received all the legal documents for Beacon Career, our company, while I was in the U.S. I told her that was the reason the farewell party was important, which let everybody experience and release their emotions. She could slowly get rid of all the documents, and that was her journey. In the U.S., I also registered a company called Beacon Career, just like the one I had before.

Finally, all the people were gone. Only Mike and I stayed in the hotel. When I stood at the high level of the building and saw Shanghai, I felt so emotional. It was time to say goodbye to this city. Since 2015, when I came to Shanghai, I have created my business to meet many like-minded collaborators. Mike and I had a wedding and a married life here. Shanghai is a special place for me, and it is a beautiful and modern city. But I had to leave. This was my journey. Thanks to this city and thanks to the people who lived in this city.

On the last day, I met my deskmate from high school. We had not seen each other for over twenty years. I felt more peaceful with my past and thanked them for their companionship during the different periods in my life. We were happy when we came together, and we weren't sad when we parted. We did not contact each other very much as we had different lives, the same as my family members. I rarely contact them. For the coaches, I knew we would not keep in touch very often. We would go in different directions, like river streams.

This farewell marked the closing of a long, meaningful chapter. I had returned to say goodbye not just to people and places but to a former version of myself. As I hugged loved ones, parted with teammates, and released tears long held in, I honored both my roots and my growth. Like a river, life keeps flowing. I cannot cling to the banks of the past. My journey now moves forward toward a wider sea—carrying the wisdom, love, and courage I gathered in China and making space for the new role I am ready to embrace. I was like an actor, and I needed to prepare for my next role.

. . .

One day, I watched an interview with famous actor Damian Lau (Chinese name: Songren Liu), who was a Catholic from Hong Kong. He shared how his spiritual director, Father Giovanni, deeply impacted him when he was young. Father Giovanni once sent the Legion of Mary, of which Damian was a member, to Tsing Yi Island for a week of evangelization work.

"After we came back, Father Giovanni had already left the parish. He didn't tell us beforehand. We felt betrayed—you sent us to work, and when we returned, you were gone. You can imagine how hurt we were. We depended on him a lot," Damian described.

Young Damian was filled with sadness and anger. He searched high and low for Father Giovanni, wanting to know why he had left without a word.

When Damian finally found him, Father Giovanni said,

"When I leave a parish, I have to forget about that parish. Otherwise, I am unfair to the parishioners in my next parish."

This remark had a deep impact on Damian.

"It's just like acting," Damian said.

"When you step into a new role, you must forget the last role you played. You can't keep saying, 'I was very successful in that role. I was this and that.' If you keep looking back, you can't move forward."

Like Damian, I knew I couldn't fully enter a new role while still holding on to the last. I had to let go.

This journey of transition went beyond leaving a country. It involved releasing old identities so I could begin again with new meaning, new creation, and a new self.

Epilogue
Three Stages of Transition in Bridges' Transition Model

D uring my transition journey, I followed William Bridges' transition model, which describes three stages of change: Endings, the Neutral Zone, and a New Beginning. Here, I'll share their importance, challenges, and solutions.

Endings
Individuals first grieve what they are letting go before adopting new ways of being.

Why is the Ending So Important?
An ending is not the final result—it is the beginning of something new. It is not an accident or a detour but a natural part of self-development that everyone must go through.

New growth cannot take root in soil still covered with old habits, attitudes, and beliefs. Endings create the space needed for transformation. Sometimes, the fear of letting go can make things feel even more chaotic, causing missed opportunities for growth and self-discovery.

What Are the Challenges of Endings?

There are five key aspects of a natural ending: disengagement, dismantling, disidentification, disenchantment, and disorientation. In short, endings involve three main detachments:

- **Environmental detachment**: leaving behind a familiar environment and relationships.
- **Identity detachment**: letting go of the role and identity tied to past experiences.
- **Separation from goals**: losing interest in old goals, leading to a period of confusion and emptiness.

The main challenges of endings include:

1. Fear of Letting Go

Endings require courage, and many struggle because they fear uncertainty and losing control.

2. The Difficulty of Disidentification

Letting go of an old identity is often the hardest part of transition. When an identity is deeply tied to work, status, or relationships, losing it can feel unsettling. This process doesn't happen automatically—it requires conscious effort.

In my transition, I once saw my identity as a Chinese entrepreneur as my greatest source of pride. The thought of losing that identity scared me. For a long time, I even resisted embracing my immigrant identity.

How can you deal with the challenges?

1. Accept the fear

Fear is a natural part of endings. Instead of rejecting it, acknowledge it. Being brave doesn't mean having no fear—it means moving forward despite it.

2. **Build a support system**

According to Schlossberg's 4S Transition Theory, support is key during transitions. Whether it's from intimate relationships (partners, spouses), family (parents, children, siblings), friends, or communities, having support makes it easier to let go.

Professional support—such as coaching, therapy, or counseling—can also be powerful in navigating change.

3. **Let Go of Old Identities and Cultivate New Ones**

One way to ease this process is by finding new role models. As an immigrant, the role models from your birth country may no longer fully support your journey. In that case, you need to look for a new role model in your adopted country. If you are from Asia, you can find role models who are Asian American, white, black, or other immigrants in the U.S.

During my transition, I found two role models, Maleficent and Iris Apfel, who were American female figures. My previous role model, Ayn Rand, was an immigrant from Russia and was successful in the U.S. She became famous through her writing. Now, I was following in her footsteps.

The Neutral Zone

Self-development requires space. This is the space to sort out the past and nurture the future.

Why Is the Neutral Zone Important?

When people break away from the original meaning, in the stage of alternation between the old and the new, they gain a kind of space, establish a connection with a deeper and broader spiritual field, and examine their lives from a more essential perspective.

Perhaps what people experience at this stage is the impermanence of Buddhism, with some transparency and compassion. Just as the bleak winter accumulates the power of spring, the period of confusion also accumulates the power of a new beginning.

The challenges for the Neutral Zone include:

1. **The urge to go back.**

The first instinct is to return to what's familiar, to abandon the transition and retreat into the past.

2. **The urge to rush forward.**

When going back is no longer an option, the next reaction is to escape the discomfort as quickly as possible, rushing into a new beginning before fully processing the change. Trying to force an ending often leads to setbacks, making the transition even longer.

To navigate the Neutral Zone, follow these steps:

1. **Understand how the brain works.**

Our brain naturally resists change, trying to pull us back into the "web of meaning" we once knew—even if it no longer fits. Instead of returning to the past, develop new routines, such as volunteering, picking up a new hobby, or exercising regularly.

2. **Surrender to the process.**

One must give in to the emptiness and stop struggling to escape it. The neutral zone is the only source of self-renewal that we all seek. We need it, just the way that an apple tree needs the cold winter.

3. **Spend time alone.**

People in transition often feel drawn to solitude. Without distractions, their spiritual awareness deepens, helping them reconnect with themselves.

4. **Release emotions.**

When you have more space, you have the awareness to observe your emotions. Try to release the emotions; some are very obvious, and some are hidden.

My transformation began in the neutral zone from March 2021 to December 2022, and even now, I sometimes revisit this phase when stepping into a new beginning.

During this time, I spent most of my days alone, deeply exploring my relationship with myself. I searched for the meaning of life, rediscovered happiness, processed emotions, reconnected with my body, and let go of negative ties to my birth country.

This phase was where I experienced the most growth. It gave me the space and time to release old energy, break past patterns, and create a new self-image.

A New Beginning

The essence of a new beginning is the reorganization process of psychological structure.

A new beginning requires the ability to tolerate change and the ability to let go of our original experiences. Sometimes, only by acknowledging the loss can we truly let go and start over.

If you don't let go of the original things, you won't see new possibilities. Giving up is not easier than persisting. It also requires courage.

We have a new identity, a new career, and a new self. We start over and become more flexible and resilient until the next change comes. It is during such difficult changes that people become profound and complex.

What are the challenges for a new beginning?

1. A new beginning is always full of surprises, and no new beginning is completely planned. This is because life itself cannot be completely planned.

2. It is important to distinguish between a real new beginning in someone's life and a simple defensive reaction to an ending. For example, some people are laid off and avoid the endings and neutral zone stages. They immediately find another job because they are very scared. This is not a true new beginning but rather a defensive reaction to the ending. Later, they may still need to face many issues, such as emotions from the previous job.

3. Even though the external new beginning may have happened very quickly, once it becomes evident, the internal re-identification and re-engagement always occur more slowly.

How do we deal with the challenges?

1. **Follow Your Heart to Necessity**

However, a new beginning has a special connection with your previous life experiences, making all of this seem like destiny. So, you see, there is a chance for a new beginning, and this chance contains necessity.

It is like there used to be many selves in you. One of the most important selves has been stripped of its own limitations, while another self that you thought was insignificant has grown up.

Because this new self conforms to your inner values and the needs of the external environment, one day, it becomes your main identity.

2. **Take Action and Own It**

Take action and begin to identify yourself with the result of the new beginning. You are the one who did it.

3. **Stop Preparing—Just Start**

If you wait until you feel "fully ready", you may never begin. Instead of focusing on the goal, shift your attention to the process. I used to set rigid deadlines, but I often struggled to meet them. Eventually, I stopped over-preparing—when I was truly ready, I simply took action.

4. **Allow Yourself Time to Transition**

Many traditional rituals acknowledge that returning from the neutral zone happens in stages. Even when external changes seem complete, the internal process continues. Be patient and gentle with yourself.

5. **Embrace the Cycle**

Endings and beginnings, emptiness and renewal—this is the rhythm of every transition in life.

The dream of becoming an author came to me when I started a new beginning.

I had dreamed of being a writer since I was young, and I had many female writers as my role models while growing up. But I didn't believe I could make it, even though I had already published a book. The writers I admired had more talent for literature and had started their writing careers earlier. I was not like that. This mindset stopped me.

In September 2023, I talked to an American coach who mentioned she was writing a book based on her real experiences. I thought I could do it too. It felt accidental, yet necessary. I started writing this book in early 2024. The more I wrote, the more I believed I could do it. Writing would become my biggest identity after my forties.

I planned to start with nonfiction, drawing from my real life. After writing eight to ten books, I would try fiction. This is a learning process. My rich life experiences and my deep understanding of people through my coaching work are precious resources for writing. Most importantly, I found my inner motivation.

In my mind, I have a picture: writing is like a river. I take a boat with my cat, Happy, a pen, and paper, allowing the river to guide me. Along the way, I visit two little girls—one from a Chinese village and the other from a Native American tribe. They stand on the banks, staring at me with curious and innocent eyes. I tell them I have come to write their stories. They live in such remote places where only my river can reach them.

They are overjoyed to share their thoughts and experiences. I write it all down, for no one else cares about their inner worlds. Now, their stories are recorded in words.

These two little girls, so ordinary yet so extraordinary, were me as a child, my mother as a child, my grandmother as a child, my sister as a child, my female friends and clients as children, Chinese women as children, American women as children, the women of this planet.

Writing is both a record and a connection, a way to honor the beauty within us and to never forget who we truly are.

In Pictures

Chapter 2: Team gathering in Shenzhen, China, in January 2020. Xiaoyun Li (second from left), Yali Yu (third from left), Esther (fifth from left).

Chapter 2: Group photo from our get-together in Shenzhen, China, in January 2020.

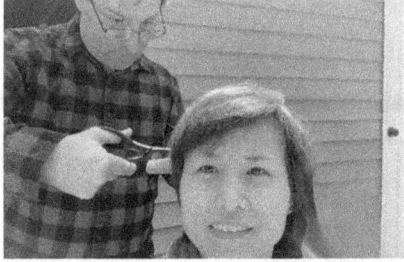

*Chapter 3: Mike cut my hair in the backyard in April 2020
when COVID-19 hit.*

*Chapter 3: Freedom (left) and Hope in May 2021. We adopted
them during the early pandemic.*

Chapter 12: The Akita dog I walked with and hugged in April 2022.

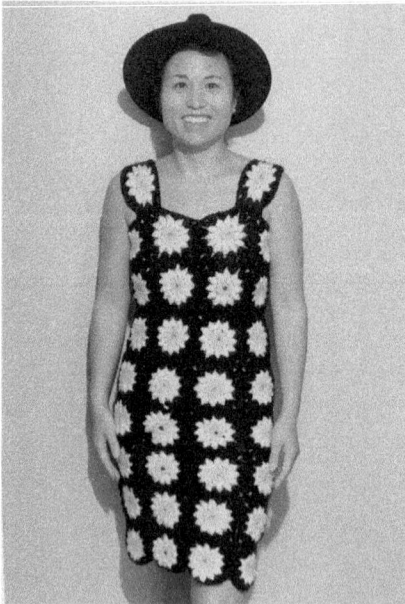

Chapter 15: The dress I crocheted in May 2023.

*Chapter 21: Esther gave a presentation at the NCDA
conference in Chicago in June 2023.*

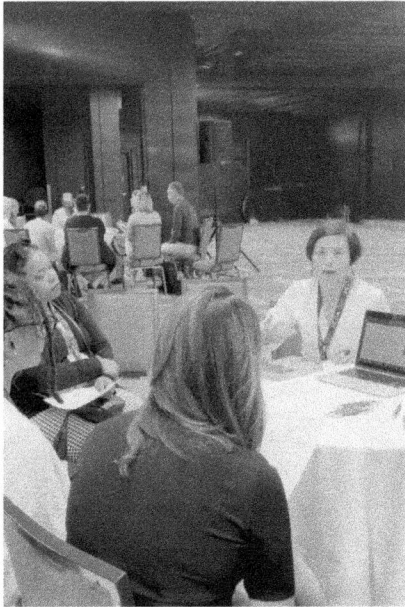

*Chapter 21: Esther presented a round table at the NCDA
conference in Chicago in June 2023.*

Chapter 23: Four coaches at ICF Converge in August 2023.
Hellen (first from the left), Esther (third from the left).

Chapter 24: Happy was on my shoulder in September 2023.

Chapter 26: Parts of author's extended family in China, in December 2023. Esther (fifth from the left).

Chapter 26: I hugged Xin Zhao in tears at our final get-together in Shanghai, China, in December 2023. Esther (first from the left).

Chapter 26: *After the tears, our team smiled and said goodbye with funny expressions in Shanghai, China, in December 2023. Left to right: Yali Yu, Esther, Lei Guo, Xiaoyun Li, Jing Wang, Xin Zhao.*

Chapter 26: *Group photo from our final get-together in Shanghai, China, in December 2023.*

Notes

Author's Note

The Alchemist by Paulo Coelho (1993)

Chapter 2

The Almanack of Naval Ravikant: A Guide to Wealth and Happiness by Eric Jorgenson (2020)

Chapter 5

Your Body Knows the Answer (《身体知道答案》) by Zhihong Wu (2013)

Spontaneously Healed: A Complete Guide to Holistic Mind–Body–Spirit Health (《不药而愈：身心灵整体健康完全讲义》) by Yiren Wang (2010)

Chapter 6

Power vs. Force: The Hidden Determinants of Human Behavior by David R. Hawkins (2002)

Heartland, Season 5, Episode 1: "Finding Freedom" (CBC, 2011)

Chapter 7

Busting Loose from the Business Game by Robert Scheinfeld (2009)

Quote: "This, too, will pass" from *A New Earth: Awakening to Your Life's Purpose* by Eckhart Tolle (2005)

Chapter 8

Siddhartha by Hermann Hesse (1922)

The Book of Joy by the Dalai Lama, Desmond Tutu, and Douglas Abrams (2016)

Chapter 10

The Art of Happiness: A Handbook for Living by Howard C. Cutler and the Dalai Lama (1998)

Emotional Balance: The Path to Inner Peace and Harmony by Roy Martina (2010)

Conversations with God (Book 1) by Neale Donald Walsch (1995)

A New Earth: Awakening to Your Life's Purpose by Eckhart Tolle (2005)

Chapter 11

Emotional Balance: The Path to Inner Peace and Harmony by Roy Martina (2010)

The Book of Joy by the Dalai Lama, Desmond Tutu, and Douglas Abrams (2016)

Chapter 12

Emotional Balance: The Path to Inner Peace and Harmony by Roy Martina (2010)

Chapter 14

Outliers: The Story of Success by Malcolm Gladwell (2008)

Counseling Adults in Transition: Linking Schlossberg's Theory with Practice in a Diverse World by Nancy K. Schlossberg, Elinor B. Waters, and Jane Goodman (4th ed. 2019)

Chapter 16

The Clear English Academy by Keenyn Rhodes—English training resource

The Brain That Changes Itself by Norman Doidge (2007)

Chapter 21

Leaky House—Real Methods and Misconceptions in English Learning (《漏屋—英语学习的真实方法及误区分析》)— blog post

The Scent of Desire by Rachel Herz (2016)

Anthony Bourdain: No Reservations, Season 5, Episode 13—Chicago (TV series)

Chapter 24

Coraline film directed by Henry Selick (2009)

Chapter 25

Quote: "Master of life is the opposite of control" from *A New Earth: Awakening to Your Life's Purpose* by Eckhart Tolle (2005)

Chapter 26

Career Development and Counseling: Putting Theory and Research to Work by Steven D. Brown and Robert W. Lent (1st ed. 2005)

The Heroine's Journey by Maureen Murdock (1990)

Quote from Damian Lau in *St. Francis of Assisi Musical: Close Encounters with Damian Lau*—YouTube

Epilogue

Transitions: Making Sense of Life's Changes, Revised 25th Anniversary Edition by William Bridges (2004)

Recommended Resources

Books for Career Development

- *Working Identity: Unconventional Strategies for Reinventing Your Career*—Herminia Ibarra
- *The Long View: Career Strategies to Start Strong, Reach High, and Go Far*—Brian Fetherstonhaugh
- *What Color is Your Parachute?*—Richard Nelson Bolles
- *Now, Discover Your Strengths*—Marcus Buckingham & Donald O. Clifton
- *Transitions: Making Sense of Life's Changes*—William Bridges
- *Awakening: Design Your Life to Be the Way You Want*（《觉醒: 把人生设计成你想要的样了》）—Hong Wang

Books for Self-Exploration

- *Type Talk: The 16 Personality Types That Determine How We Live, Love, and Work*—Otto Kroeger
- *Please Understand Me: Character and Temperament Types*—David Keirsey

• *The Introvert Advantage: How to Thrive in an Extrovert World*—Marti Olsen Laney

• *Highly Sensitive People in an Insensitive World: How to Create a Happy Life*—Ilse Sand

Books for Self-Growth

• *Mindset: Changing the Way You Think to Fulfill Your Potential*—Dr. Carol Dweck

• *Humankind: A Hopeful History*—Rutger Bregman

• *Outliers: The Story of Success*—Malcolm Gladwell

• *The Road Less Traveled*—M. Scott Peck

• *The Courage to Be Disliked: How to Free Yourself, Change Your Life, and Achieve Real Happiness*—Ichiro Kishimi & Fumitake Koga

Books for Energy, Health & Emotional Well-being

• *Power vs. Force*—David R. Hawkins

• *Emotional Balance: The Path to Inner Peace and Harmony*—Roy Martina

• *Spontaneously Healed: A Complete Guide to Holistic Mind–Body–Spirit Health* (《不药而愈: 身心灵整体健康完全讲义》) Yiren Wang

• *You Can Heal Your Life*—Louise Hay

• *Heal Your Body*—Louise Hay

Books for Happiness & Spirituality

• *The Art of Happiness: A Handbook for Living*—Howard Cutler

• *The Book of Joy*—The Dalai Lama, Desmond Tutu, and Douglas Abrams

• *A New Earth: Awakening to Your Life's Purpose*—Eckhart Tolle

• *Siddhartha*—Hermann Hesse

Books for Career Women
• *Playing Big: Practical Wisdom for Women Who Want to Speak Up, Create, and Lead*—Tara Mohr
• *I Wish I'd Known This: 6 Career-Accelerating Secrets for Women Leaders*—Brenda Wensil & Kathryn Heath
• *How Women Rise: Break the 12 Habits Holding You Back from Your Next Raise, Promotion, or Job*—Sally Helgesen & Marshall Goldsmith
• *The Signature of All Things*—Elizabeth Gilbert
• *The Heroine's Journey*—Maureen Murdock

Inspirational Movies
• *Soul* (USA)
• *Inside Out* (USA)
• *Good Will Hunting* (USA)
• *Dead Poets Society* (USA)
• *Forrest Gump* (USA)
• *The Shawshank Redemption* (USA)
• *The Pursuit of Happiness* (USA)
• *8 Mile* (USA)
• *To Kill a Mockingbird* (USA)
• *A Beautiful Mind* (USA)
• *The Truman Show* (USA)
• *Cinema Paradiso* (Italy)
• *The Chorus* (France/Switzerland/Germany)
• *The Legend of 1900* (Italy)
• *Slumdog Millionaire* (India)
• *3 Idiots* (India)
• *Like Stars on Earth* (India)
• *The Horse Whisperer* (USA)

- *Seabiscuit* (USA)
- *My Father and My Son* (Turkey)

Inspirational Movies Featuring Strong Female Leads
- *Cruella* (USA—Disney)
- *Maleficent* (USA—Disney)
- *Turning Red* (USA/Canada—Pixar, Disney)
- *Lemon Tree (Etz Limon)* (Israel)
- *Desert Flower* (Germany/UK/Austria)
- *Erin Brockovich* (USA)
- *Homeless to Harvard: The Liz Murray Story* (USA)
- *Freedom Writers* (USA)
- *Million Dollar Baby* (USA)
- *Te Ata* (USA)
- *Amélie* (France)
- *Battle for Sevastopol* (Russia/Ukraine)

Inspirational Female-Lead TV Shows & Dramas
- *The Queen's Gambit* (USA)
- *Anne with an E* (Canada)

About the Author

Esther Wang is a seasoned career coach with 15 years of experience. With her rich multicultural background, she supports clients from diverse cultural and professional backgrounds. She specializes in areas such as career transitions, international relocation, immigrant adjustment, leadership development, emotional regulation, imposter syndrome, promotions and career advancement, personal branding, entrepreneurial mindset, business building, life purpose, cross-cultural collaboration, and the career development of first-generation immigrants.

Esther holds a PCC credential (2021) from the International Coaching Federation (ICF) and is a Certified Master of Career Services (2022) accredited by the National Career Development Association (NCDA).

She is the author of *Awakening: Design Your Life to Be the Way You Want* (2018) and an experienced presenter. Her speaking engagements include topics such as "Empowering Women to Overcome Their Imposter Syndrome," "Using Mantras to Move Clients from Insecurity to Confidence" (2023), and the co-presentation "Cultural Competence in Career Counseling: Empowering Asian Immigrants and International Students" in 2024 at the Global Career Development Conference by NCDA.

Esther began her private coaching practice in 2016. Throughout this journey, she harnessed her entrepreneurial spirit, leading a team of six women to provide career coaching, training independent career coaches, and offering online career development and self-improvement courses—impacting thousands. She is the founder of Beacon Career.

A passionate explorer, Esther has lived in Beijing, Shanghai, and North Carolina, and volunteered in Malawi, Africa. She has traveled to 20 countries across five continents and visited more than 35 U.S. states, often planning her own adventures.

Born and raised in China, Esther immigrated to the U.S. in 2019 at the age of 39. She now lives in Charlotte, North Carolina, with her British husband and their two cats, Freedom and Happy.

Connect with Esther:
    estherwangcoaching@gmail.com
    www.linkedin.com/in/estherwangcareercoach

www.ingramcontent.com/pod-product-compliance
Lightning Source LLC
La Vergne TN
LVHW041213080426
835508LV00011B/943